**BRING YOUR BIG ENERGY**

# BRING YOUR BIG ENERGY

## IGNITE THE AUTHENTIC POWER WITHIN YOU

**STACEY KULONGOWSKI**

MANUSCRIPTS
PRESS

MANUSCRIPTS PRESS

COPYRIGHT © 2024 STACEY KULONGOWSKI
*All rights reserved.*

BRING YOUR BIG ENERGY
*Ignite the Authentic Power within You*

ISBN    979-8-88926-195-7  *Paperback*
        979-8-88926-196-4  *Hardcover*
        979-8-88926-194-0  *Ebook*

*To my beautiful daughters,*
*Grace, Madeline, and Charlotte,*
*May you always Bring Your Big Energy and*
*unapologetically live your most authentic life.*

*To my Mom and Dad,*
*For always believing in and encouraging me to*
*use my Big Energy to change the world.*

*To my husband, Eric,*
*For embracing my Big Energy, no matter*
*how it shined in each season.*

The tree that never had to fight
For sun and sky and air and light,
But stood out in the open plain
And always got its share of rain,
Never became a forest king
But lived and died a scrubby thing.

The man who never had to toil
To gain and farm his patch of soil,
Who never had to win his share
Of sun and sky and light and air,
Never became a manly man
But lived and died as he began.

Good timber does not grow with ease,
The stronger wind, the stronger trees,
The further sky, the greater length,
The more the storm, the more the strength.

By sun and cold, by rain and snow,
In trees and men good timbers grow.

Where thickest lies the forest growth
We find the patriarchs of both.
And they hold counsel with the stars
Whose broken branches show the scars
Of many winds and much of strife.

This is the common law of life.

Douglas Malloch, 1922, Good Timber

# Contents

|  | INTRODUCTION | 9 |
|---|---|---|
| CHAPTER 1. | HOW DID YOU GET HERE, AND WHERE IS HERE? | 23 |
| CHAPTER 2. | SPARK ENERGY TRANSFORMATION PROCESS | 41 |
| CHAPTER 3. | SELF-REFLECTION | 51 |
| CHAPTER 4. | PURPOSE | 77 |
| CHAPTER 5. | ABANDON (AND UNPLUG) | 101 |
| CHAPTER 6. | RESULTS | 129 |
| CHAPTER 7. | KINETIC ENERGY | 159 |
| CHAPTER 8. | BRING YOUR BIG "LEADER" ENERGY | 185 |
| CHAPTER 9. | EMBRACE YOUR EPIC ENERGY | 207 |
|  | ACKNOWLEDGMENTS | 219 |
|  | NOTES | 225 |

# INTRODUCTION

---

*"Success is liking yourself, liking what you do, and liking how you do it."*

—MAYA ANGELOU

In 2022, I lost my job, my identity, my sanity, and myself. Surprisingly, these tragedies brought me incredible clarity and ended up being some of the most phenomenal blessings of my life.

Theoretically, I had it all: the impressive tech job, the big house, the fancy car, and ample family vacation time. Although I was living what many have come to believe is the "right" dream, it came with intense amounts of stress, some pretty tight golden handcuffs, and a sense of suffocation under the weight of it all.

In losing what I thought was "having it all," I finally reached a point so intense that I knew I needed to make some major changes. It took being almost completely broken to realize I needed a full-blown rebuild. Through this challenging journey of self-reconstruction, I emerged stronger and more fulfilled than ever before. Once I realized what could be possible for me on the other side, I knew there would be no turning back for me. Now, I feel called to share what I've learned—with the hope that you, too, can find that same joy and fulfillment in your life.

Before what I have come to call my biggest "Intensity Point," my bright yellow energy was all but extinguished from years of working to the point of burnout and still feeling like I was never enough. I was buckling under the pressure of sales quotas while doing my best to motivate a team against impossible odds and maintain a tight-knit culture in a virtual setting. I was struggling as a leader, as a mom, and as a human. What had always brought me success and security before was simply no longer working.

And it sucked—because I had no one to blame but myself. I had expended my energies in all the wrong places. I was so focused on proving that I had all the answers, that I could solve the unsolvable and was living a picture-perfect life, that I was completely missing the point.

It took some time to come to terms with it, but I eventually realized that this life no longer fit me—nor I it.

At this point, the universe introduced me to the notion of an Intensity Point. An Intensity Point is that moment, or series of smaller moments, along your life path when your perspective is so fundamentally changed that you question everything. You can no longer continue down your well-worn road as it is no longer serving you.

I had been there before—in a similar place of defeat, loss, and the unknown. In 2016, at age forty-two, I was diagnosed with breast cancer. Luckily, it was detected early, and I had an amazing medical team supporting me in my healing. I was extremely fortunate to sail through multiple surgeries and navigate the radiation treatment smoothly.

At the same time, I was also too caught up in keeping it all moving up and to the right to slow down for even a moment. Throughout the entire treatment process, I never took a single day off work. I just continued to push down all of my fears and worries while at the same time excelling at work, one promotion after another. During my eight weeks of radiation, I would head into the hospital, get burned, get dressed, and go to the office to lead my teams with confidence and grace each day while at the same time struggling physically and emotionally. Survival mode was all I knew, and I thought it was serving me well.

The following eight months were pure hell as I endured the hormone therapy drug used to treat and prevent recurring cancer. Although my oncologist denied any connection, I suffered from a list of twenty-two side effects, ranging from a total body rash to multi-limb numbness. In the end, I advocated for myself and chose to end my treatment—finally closing the door on my cancer journey. It was a transformative experience, and only those who have walked the path can truly comprehend how cancer and the healing process can leave you forever damaged.

You would think cancer treatment would have given me existential perspective and introspection, but life has a funny way of defying expectations. Eventually, time passed, and it was all behind me. Without even realizing it, I fell back into my old habits of constant activity, grinding at work, and doing whatever it took to keep my life running smoothly. I never afforded myself the ability to be "in it." I just wanted to get through it.

Although life-altering, I was unwilling to accept that I would be forever changed. I learned the hard way that when you don't allow yourself time to process, the pain has nowhere to go but deeper inside you.

My friend Kim, a fellow survivor and badass mama, says, "A scar has the beauty of remembrance and reflection that an open wound does not." She's right. Only when we have that space to pause and honor our experience are we able to move forward. Given how petrified I was of being pitied, worried that the Big C would become my entire identity, I only shared my pain and story with a handful of close friends.

After I spent some time feeling sorry for myself, almost two years if we're counting, I was back and better than ever by 2019. Pre-pandemic me was living her best existence—physically, emotionally, and spiritually. It had taken me standing at the edge of life, wondering if it would end abruptly, to build one that brought me incredible joy.

And then, the pandemic hit, and everything changed. Through the quarantined and confusing years that followed, we cherished some of our most amazing family memories together. However, my corporate stress continued to escalate daily until I was eventually living in a complete pressure cooker.

The weight of suppressing my cancer ordeal combined with the chaos of our unknown world unleashed a torrent of emotions within me, triggering a deep state of post-traumatic stress disorder (PTSD). I had no idea such a thing even existed, but I now know this happens when you stack new trauma on top of unresolved trauma. I can best describe it as feeling that you are incredibly out of control, like your existence is meaningless and you are operating in a constant state of fight or flight.

I will never forget the look of concern on my therapist's face when she shared my PTSD test results with me. "You scored at the severe level," she explained. "These scores are in line with what I see in my Vietnam veteran clients."

I was completely stunned. I could feel each and every one of those points on that scale carving deeper into my soul. Although I would never suggest that my hardships and life experiences are comparable to those of my esteemed score sharers, the emotional and mental fallout were incredibly similar and equally profound.

To make things worse, my brother and his wife, whose wedding I had officiated, were getting divorced after eleven years of marriage. In addition to the loss I felt for our family, I was forced to say goodbye to my sister-in-law. She had been my ride-or-die for the past fifteen years. We parented together, commiserated together, laughed together, and always joked that we were raising our six kids as siblings, not cousins. Although I am blessed to have many beautiful, caring friendships, few knew me at the same depth that she did. No matter the challenge, obstacle, or celebration, she was always there to make the best of every situation.

I was at the epitome of success but living with so many demons, and I felt like the saddest, loneliest person on the planet.

And then, the final nail in the coffin came. My most profound Intensity Point hit in March of 2022. I was navigating a pretty tumultuous revenue call trying to articulate our plan to turn our business around. The sales team I had built—and had been leading for almost a decade—was struggling to bounce back from the economic fallout related to the pandemic. While the United States and other countries were finally rebounding, my team in Canada continued to struggle.

As a leader, I had literally tried every lever available to me to motivate the team and achieve our sales quotas with limited sustainable success. It was a continual process of strategic deep dives, action planning, and constant adjustments to achieve the growth numbers we needed.

In this call, like many prior that year, I felt attacked, burned out, and out of sync with the values that were critical for me. Those deep values of trust, hard work, and integrity no longer felt appreciated by my company. I had never felt more like a failure in my life. I could not get it right. I no longer had solutions to bring, as they were falling on deaf ears and nothing was moving the needle, regardless of the amount of work or worry I invested.

For once, I couldn't solve the problem. Throughout the call, I had to take the hits while holding back my tears. The virtual room was filled with all my favorite and most admired director peers, who were reaching out and texting me with compassion as I felt my career collapsing. It felt like a total underwear-in-school moment unfolding before my eyes.

After the call ended, I closed my laptop feeling shell-shocked. At a total loss, I sat paralyzed in my chair for a full five minutes just staring at the blank screen. Slowly, I began to sink down to the floor—shaking uncontrollably. Feeling the weight of a thousand pounds on my shoulders, I wrapped myself in a blanket and spent the next hour sobbing under my desk. Short of the loss of a relative or my first broken heart, I had never felt so deeply and incredibly sad.

After a lifetime of hustling, always the overachiever and problem-solver, the one everyone leaned on for advice, I had hit a wall. I had nothing left in the tank, mentally running on fumes. Even now, almost two years later, thinking back to that version of myself, utterly shattered, makes me sick to my stomach. It hurts to realize I let things get that bad without listening to my body. If I could go back, I would just hold her and tell her it was all going to be okay.

In retrospect, I was broken down and knew I needed to do something drastic. What I did next, at the time, felt so weak and embarrassing. But now with time and perspective, I want to tell that version of me that what she did was incredibly courageous, and I am so proud of her for taking the terrifying unknown path forward. I did something I never thought I could. I took a mental health leave from my big corporate job to focus on healing. What I initially thought would be a week or two off to clear my head ended up being a therapist-mandated six-month leave.

Taking this leave eventually granted me the clarity to realize how inauthentically I was living. This opportunity to heal, reflect, and rebuild propelled me into building my own transformative process, altering my life permanently. Although I cherish all of my past experiences and memories, transitioning from an achievement-focused life to one centered on serving others is 100 percent where I am meant to be. Guiding others to transform their lives and align with their values, energy, and passion is where I belong. To say I feel blessed and fortunate that I found my way here doesn't even begin to capture it.

However, rebuilding something so broken did not happen overnight. I grappled with sadness, shame, and anger. I felt lost, unsure of where life was taking me, and every step felt like a struggle. Yet amid the uncertainty, I immersed myself in therapy—pushing the boundaries of self-discovery.

In addition, each month I became a canvas for reconstructing my shattered life, one mindful stroke at a time. From embracing the solace of yoga to conquering a half marathon, and from cherishing moments with loved ones to finding escape in books and reflection, I poured my soul into every part of it.

It wasn't until nearly six months later, as I sat in quiet reflection atop the majestic Berkshires mountains at the Kripalu Center for Yoga & Health, that I realized my life was forever changed. On that breathtaking morning, as the remnants of the night rain burned off and disappeared into the tops of the trees below me, a glimmer of sunlight pierced through the clouds, illuminating the valley below. In that moment, I found peace, and for the first time in weeks, maybe months, I radiated hope and inspiration for what the future might hold for me.

It was a sign of a way forward again, a sign that I could rediscover my Big Energy and a new version of my authentic self—one that had been broken but now was being repaired and would come back even stronger. My battle scars would serve as a reminder of my courage to do the work. I had hit my Intensity Point, undergone an energy transformation, and was ready to spend my energy currency in ways that would give, not take life from me.

I don't think my story is rare, nor an anomaly. People are leaving their jobs at some of the highest rates in history to pursue lives of purpose. We are in an epidemic of individuals reaching their Intensity Points through burnout and layoffs and starving for what comes next as they explore transformation.

We are rooted in a society that believes success is up and to the right. We define winning as having more—more power, more money, more things. When we lack the personal clarity to chase what we want, we chase what others say we should. This exercise leaves us incredibly unfulfilled, and when we get to the top of the mountain, reach a point of intensity caused by trauma, or live through scary life experiences, we start to notice.

These kinds of events call into question the paths we have blindly followed, but as the motivational speaker and author Tony Robbins says: "Change happens when the pain of staying the same is greater than the pain of change."[1]

You are here because you are ready to make that change, and I hope I can help support and guide you on that journey.

This book delves into the concept of "Intensity Points," those pivotal moments in life when a person realizes the necessity of making a significant change. I'll guide you in intentionally shaping a vision for the life you desire and cultivating the courage to allocate your energy wisely.

I felt compelled to write this book for the very reason you're here—because nothing like it exists. Throughout my journey, I was constantly searching for a blend of meaningful real-world stories, practical exercises, and tools to guide my transformation. I needed to know I wasn't alone, find the courage to make significant changes, hear from others living bold unconventional lives, and gain the tools to take action.

*Bring Your Big Energy* is also built on the backbone of my three decades of professional experience, training, custom-built vision, and transformational workshops and research I have invested in along the way. My goal with this book is to deliver some of that magic directly to you, showing you exactly how to transition from your Intensity Point to a state of true energy fulfillment.

As we embark on this journey together, I'm committed to sharing the details of my own personal experiences. I'm also honored to present powerful stories from brave individuals who are willing to share their lessons with us.

As an executive coach and leader, I've invested thousands of hours not only in helping others transform but also in learning what strategies are effective for achieving and maintaining these life changes. When we hit these Intensity Points, our perspective changes profoundly. We become altered, challenged, inspired, and internally motivated in ways we've never experienced before—a true yin and yang experience.

For some, this means scaling the peak of success only to find emptiness despite having everything. For others, it means grappling with burnout or emerging from the aftermath of trauma. Yet in every instance, a catalyst drives us toward an energy shift.

My book offers you a five-step SPARK Energy Transformation Process to rediscover clarity after reaching your Intensity Point.

Along the way on this SPARK process, I have included a series of exercises designed to guide you. To make these moments even more engaging, each exercise will be introduced with the phrase "Ignite the Spark." This prompt will serve as your powerful call to action and align perfectly with the energy-driven theme of this journey. By "Igniting the Spark," you're not only completing an exercise, but you're fueling your personal growth with purpose, passion, and the kinetic energy to create meaningful change.

This book is perfect for those standing on the edge of their Intensity Point, craving insight into real transformation and how to achieve it. This book is for adventurous souls ready to try new things and grow. It's for people who understand that once you hit your Intensity Point, there's no going back. This book is for those who are willing to roll up their sleeves, step outside of their comfort zones, and step into their most authentic selves, maximizing their energy potential along the way.

Through these deep and sometimes provocative stories, I hope to lift the veil of shame you may be experiencing, give you that glimmer of inspiration you need to get started, and prove to you that you are walking alongside others in a community.

In the following chapters, I hope to inspire you to realize that a brighter, more fulfilling future awaits you—if you have the courage and openness to experiment.

We will enter our work together by reflecting on what got us here and where here is. We will then gain clarity on our purpose and vision while focusing on unplugging energy drainers and sparking energy sources that light us up. Lastly, we will work to uncover the results we desire and build a system to achieve a life of sustainable energy—stepping into the power of owning our story and living authentically.

We will walk through this process from a view of the vast abundance of opportunities and what-ifs, including the exploration of several possible paths, because life is not linear, nor should our exploration be.

And not to worry—in the end, we will also help you to find our Energy Hype Squad and show you how to become an energy magnet in all you do.

Are you ready to Ignite that Spark and explore the endless possibilities of living your most authentic life?

CHAPTER 1

# HOW DID YOU GET HERE, AND WHERE IS HERE?

---

*"Now that I'm here, where am I?"*

—JANIS JOPLIN

You are reading this book for a reason. You are looking for something—most likely answers on how to live your best life and optimize your energy currency. That is awesome, my friend, and I promise we will get there.

But first, we need to take a minute to talk about how you got here. I firmly believe in order to move forward, we need to reflect on where we came from. The experiences that have shaped us along the way and the impact they have on how we move forward are critical to unpack.

In order to ask the question regarding how we got here, we need to understand where "here" is. Is it the messy middle, are we lost, are we struggling, are we reborn, recalibrating? Or potentially all of those things?

We have reached that Intensity Point—meaning we have recognized our need to pivot, are willing to push through our fears, and are ready to give in to our insatiable hunger to find clarity.

As I mentioned in the introduction, an Intensity Point is a moment when something significant happens, shifting your perspective so dramatically that it makes you question your current life path. You might find yourself suddenly reflecting on where the last ten years went, feeling stuck on a never-ending treadmill, or losing touch with the present moment.

This could leave you feeling disenchanted with life, isolated, or like a victim of circumstance. At this point you start to question what comes next in ways you hadn't considered before. You're no longer relying solely on adrenaline; instead, you're focusing on using your energy and resources with greater intention.

At this point I see clients leaving high-powered executive jobs to spend more time with their kids, explore a life of adventure, or just slow down to enjoy the fruits of their labor. The stories I'll share with you feature unconventional yet life-affirming choices. They encompass darkness and light, twists and turns, sadness, joy, reinvention, and many other perspective-shifting lessons. These Intensity Points are dramatic, and maybe even a little scary, but always energizing and worth it on the other side.

Through thousands of interviews and coaching calls, I have uncovered multitudes of Intensity Points leading clients, friends, and other people to hunger for an energy transformation. It is not realistic to think I can cover them all, but I would love to share a few Intensity Points I see most often.

## CIRCUMSTANCES BEYOND OUR CONTROL

Circumstances beyond our control can have an undeniable power to reshape our perspective on life. Whether it's the sudden loss of a loved one, being laid off, navigating an illness, or surviving a natural disaster, these occurrences force us to confront the unpredictable nature of our existence.

In the face of such events, our world view perspectives are called into question as we grapple with newfound uncertainties and vulnerabilities. These events and instances create seismic shifts in our perspectives on the world, reshaping priorities, values, and perceptions in profound ways.

For my friend Adele, experiencing three significant Intensity Points all within a year drastically impacted her life focus. She sustained a head injury, learned of her sister-in-law's cancer diagnosis, and served on the front lines as a healthcare leader during COVID-19.

Her first Intensity Point had been building for years, fueled by the demands of raising children and her type A drive as a healthcare leader, always on the move to keep everything running smoothly. But overnight, everything changed when a trip and fall led to post-concussion syndrome (PCS). Six months of mandated brain rest forced her to reset, shift her focus to slow down, and be more present in treasuring each precious life moment.

Unfortunately, this newfound pace was not sustainable. A few short months later, she returned to work while at the same time learning that her best friend and sister-in-law had been diagnosed with bone cancer. This required a prolonged hospital stay and extensive knee surgery. Adele balanced being her sister-in-law's primary advocate, navigating the hospital system, and working while still dealing with headaches and brain fog from PCS.

Then, the pandemic began. The next six months became an absolute blur, and while the rest of the world slowed down and created family time, her resolution to do so evaporated. She was back on the hamster wheel within minutes.

It took one final Intensity Point, involving a close family member, to bring her to her breaking point. Only then was she able to make the consistent and life-altering changes the universe had been trying to convince her to make.

Adele sought guidance from peers like me and professionals in behavioral health. She learned strategies and lessons that we will explore in this book and slowly reframed her life again. Her perspective and priorities shifted as she slowed her pace and prioritized her self-care, family, and friends. She attended several of my transformational vision workshops, where she found peace through intentional reflection, refocusing, and energy auditing.

Despite facing multiple Intensity Points, Adele is deeply grateful for how she was able to learn, adapt, and grow from the painful and challenging circumstances that were beyond her control. Today, she enjoys a beautiful life on the other side of those experiences.

In the end, these experiences compel us to embrace change, adapt to new realities, and find meaning in the midst of chaos. They serve as powerful forces that shape our character, deepen our perspectives, and inspire us to find purpose.

After all, we cannot control what happens to us, but we can decide how we react to it and what comes next. There is so much power in something being "for us" versus happening "to us."

## BURNOUT

Marie planned to sleep on the five-hour flight from Los Angeles to Philadelphia. As a senior partner at a large professional services firm, she was no stranger to extensive work and travel. In an effort to prove herself, and show her partners her worth, she had been pulling all-nighters to prepare for her upcoming cross-country meeting. She just needed a few hours to catch up on sleep and she would be presentation ready. It had worked for her time and time again as she continued to climb to the top, so she boarded the plane feeling like she had a solid plan of attack.

Yet just as she settled in and prepared for her first shut-eye in days, a bustle of activity began all around her. Moments later, she realized what was happening. A fellow passenger was having a heart attack. As she retold the story, she was embarrassed to admit that her initial reaction was that of sheer annoyance. What nerve! Now there was no way she would be able to catch up on her sleep.

Unfortunately, the heart attack was terminal, and it led to her plane rerouting to Denver, with the poor victim leaving in a body bag. Marie did not sleep a wink. At wits' end, she finally arrived at the office incredibly rattled. Still determined to show up well, she got pumped up on caffeine and launched into her prepared presentation to her C-suite clients.

At the same time, she became acutely aware that other than the support staff, she was the only female, and certainly the only female partner, in the room, making her even more determined to keep her fatigue and stress at bay.

But then, her body betrayed her, and the worst thing she could imagine happened. Her heart began to pound, she began sweating profusely, goosebumps covered her entire body, and her breath quickened. She felt an intense pain creep up her left arm.

"There I was in front of my most esteemed clients and colleagues, and I was having a heart attack. All I could think about was how embarrassing this was going to be," Marie shared. "The rest was a blur, as our Human Resources Director swept me away to the emergency room at the local hospital."

Ultimately, and thankfully, when her diagnosis came in, it was not a heart attack—just an intense warning sign. What had begun as her body whispering for her to slow down ended up with it screaming at her via way of a massive panic attack. Her burnout had caught up with her.

The lack of self-care, sleep, and restoration had depleted her. The regular rhythm that she had become accustomed to—of overwhelming stress and emotional exhaustion coupled with the intense flight and view of her fellow passenger's heart attack—had triggered her episode.

I share her story because although society often treats burnout as a badge of honor, living with it can have severe, debilitating effects that unexpectedly impact our health and well-being. It can also have lasting negative consequences.

Burnout continues to become increasingly pervasive in the corporate world, with a significant percentage of employees reporting symptoms. In fact, a recent Gallup poll discovered that 76 percent, or roughly three out of four employees, have experienced workplace burnout.[1]

In fact, a study done by Zippia found that levels as high as 89 percent of workers have experienced burnout within the past year. In a corporate world that was already a pressure cooker of chasing results and climbing the ladder, the pandemic and the shift to remote work only contributed to additional heightened levels of stress.[2]

People are enjoying less vacation time, working more hours, trying to take on additional work left behind by their laid-off colleagues, and spending less time with family. An alarming 46 percent of US workers who receive paid time off from their employer do not take what is offered, according to a recent Pew Research Center survey.[3] This robs them of the ability to restore and recharge their energy, and instead they live at a heightened sense of speed at all times.

A large majority of my clients work in industries such as healthcare, education, tech, and consulting—where they face the highest levels of burnout possible given the demands of their jobs (long hours, high pressure, constant change).

This leads them to totally shift their perspectives and begin to reassess what truly matters, prioritize their well-being for the first time in years, and start to reimagine a new career and life ahead.

As we learned from Marie's story, burnout can lead to some pretty nasty stuff. Other ailments include decreased motivation, fatigue, chronic insomnia, anxiety, and difficulty focusing, which take a toll on both physical health and mental well-being.

In the search of wanting more and doing more, ironically, we become too depleted to enjoy it all and are incredibly removed from living the authentic life we yearn for.

**TRAUMA**
Kim's story is one of stacked trauma upon trauma. At age thirty-four, she was diagnosed with stage three breast cancer. Stunned and grieving but still propelling forward, Kim underwent surgeries and treatments. While fighting for her

own survival, she was also caring for her sick parents before losing them both to cancer.

But her journey is one of courage, reinvention, and thriving against all odds. I am honored to share her story and metamorphosis—turning tragedy into inspiration.

I first met Kim when she took the stage as a keynote speaker at a local women's event. I knew instantly that we were meant to connect—given our stories and outlooks. We both embraced the idea of transforming an Intensity Point in life into a meaningful purpose and calling.

Kim did not just survive her cancer diagnosis but used her altered perspective to reinvent herself and thrive. She captured everything she'd learned in her vulnerable and powerful book *Walk through Fire* and uses her platform as a keynote speaker to elevate the struggles and triumphs of the disease.

She also coaches others to find their purpose, runs a small business with some epic "fight cancer" merchandise, and leads her own nonprofit Survivors Corner with a mission to provide resources and services that impact the world and create positive change. Her Intensity Point is behind her now, but it served as a powerful catalyst for transformation, purpose, and change.[4]

The American Psychological Association defines trauma as an emotional response to a terrible event like an accident, crime, natural disaster, physical or emotional abuse, neglect, experiencing or witnessing violence, death of a loved one, war, and more.[5]

In fact, as a cancer survivor myself, I know trauma changes you forever, both during the experience and as you work through the lasting effects.

And to make it even more complex to understand, trauma is a deeply subjective experience; what may be traumatic for one person may not be for another.

When going through trauma, many of us feel completely alone, like we are losing our mind and are unsure of how to cope. It impacts our nervous system by activating the body's stress response system, leading to a frequent heightened state of arousal causing anxiety, hypervigilance, and difficulty concentrating.

Trauma survivors also develop triggers that cause strong emotional and physiological reactions, leading to panic attacks or flashbacks and decreased trust of self and others. As was my case, when stacking traumas, people can develop post-traumatic stress disorder (PTSD) or other mental health conditions.

It has a large impact on self-identity, confidence levels, and how people see themselves, causing guilt, shame, and questioning their own worth and capabilities. This gives them a warped view of the predictability of the world and results in a more cautious or pessimistic outlook, holding survivors back from embracing a more full life. The impact of trauma is real.

But there is hope, as you will see through many of the stories in this book. By acknowledging and working through it, we can transform pain into a catalyst for growth, so you can live your best life by leveraging your lessons learned and experiences to help and inspire others.

## CHANGES OF HEART

The King family call themselves the Five Traveling Kings. Their change of heart led Jen, Dave, and their three children (kindergarten, third, and sixth grade) to take an entire year off to travel around the world.

A "change of heart" is an event entirely driven by you. It's not influenced by outside forces and often challenges conventional expectations. These changes come from lifelong dreams that have been dormant until they suddenly awaken. That nagging feeling emerges in a certain season of life when you're questioning what's next. These unconventional urges grow stronger over time until you can no longer ignore them, pulling you in a new direction.

The Kings' trip arose as a dream that began twenty years prior when the two young and adventurous newlyweds traveled the world on their own. They loved exploring new cultures, food, and traditions while living a life of adventure. As time went on and they built their lives and careers, they often entertained the idea of someday having a family. If they were blessed with children, they wanted to share an immersive international experience with them.

And then the day finally arrived. The time just felt right. They took the plunge to explore the world because their change of heart was so strong, they could no longer ignore it. Yes, it would take a significant amount of money and logistics. It would be scary, complicated, and let's be honest, a bit "out there," but they just knew it was meant to be. They predicted this adventure would be a core memory for their kids and life-altering for them as a family. And wow, they sure were right.

As Jen shared her story with me, I could see the passion light up in her eyes. "We realized one day that we only had our older daughter at home for five more years," she explained. "If we didn't act now, we might never find a better time. From there, it just snowballed. What did we have to lose? What could go wrong?"

Jen and Dave are both corporate professionals who spent a lifetime building successful careers—always enjoying work and play along the way. However, they had never taken prolonged time off to tackle something of this caliber. So after some careful planning, they left their jobs in big tech, packed up one suitcase each, and set out on an adventure of a lifetime—living their unconventional but beautifully full life. I could write an entire book on their adventure, or maybe they will one day. But for now if you are looking for motivation and inspiration to explore the world in a year, check them out on Instagram, @5TravelingKings. You may end up packing your suitcase tonight!

But how do you decide if this change of heart is strong enough to make a life pivot?

Jen advises: "If there's something you truly want to do, often the only thing holding you back is fear. Our approach is to write down our dream alongside the opportunity cost of not pursuing it. If the opportunity cost isn't compelling enough, we set the paper aside and move on peacefully. But with this dream, the opportunity cost of not pursuing it was too great. We knew we couldn't walk away."

Changes of heart challenge you to step outside of your comfort zone, confront your fears, and embrace vulnerability. They inspire you to pursue authenticity and alignment deep within your soul.

If this resonates with you, you are likely navigating these internal transformations, and your perspectives on life, love, and purpose are about to undergo seismic shifts—guiding you toward greater fulfillment and connection. You may not have all the answers but you are curious and asking the question: "What if?"

Ultimately, changes of heart empower you to embrace uncertainty and embark on a journey of self-discovery that redefines who you are and the path you choose to follow.

## TOP OF THE MOUNTAIN

I did all the right things. I got mostly A's at my tiny Class D school. I was inducted into the National Honor Society and graduated fourth in my class. I graduated from a Big Ten university with high honors. I got great jobs and moved all over the country to chase titles and status. I married my soulmate and had three amazing daughters. I landed a job at the best company on earth, traveled the world, led big teams, and managed billions of dollars in revenue. I climbed up the ladder to arrive at an unheard-of director level, all while secretly battling breast cancer.

My director role at Google afforded me a level of wealth that allowed for many material things and also secured a stronger future for my kids than I ever thought would be possible. I am forever grateful for the life it afforded us and for my experiences there that in so many ways molded me into the leader and person I am today.

Coming from a modest upbringing and seeing my parents struggle to make ends meet, I wanted it in what felt like a desperate way.

But it all came at a cost. I got to the top of the mountain and was exhausted, lost, frustrated, and defeated. I had it all and had done all the right things to get there. However, while the view was beautiful, it was snowy, cold, and lonely at the top. In the search for wholeness, I ended up at a hollow destination.

I longed for wholeness, the opposite of hollowness. To me, it means filling your inner void with love and purpose, freeing yourself from the need for external validation. It's about cultivating strong internal confidence, so you no longer seek approval from others. It's your path, and you choose where it leads.

This realization led me to my second career as a coach. Coaching fills my cup in ways I never knew existed. When I hold space for my clients and witness them overcoming seemingly impossible obstacles or experiencing aha moments, I feel a profound sense of wholeness. I know I am exactly where I am meant to be. The journey is no longer about me. It's about my clients and their success. I feel blessed and proud to have climbed my own mountain, but now, working in alignment with my purpose of serving others, the work I do doesn't even feel like work. That is what living authentically is all about.

In *The Myth of More* by Joseph Novello, renowned American psychiatrist, medical advisor, and author, observes how people constantly chase after happiness. However, they are often confusing happiness with pleasure, which sets them up for continual frustration and failure. They believe happiness comes from more money, more things.[6]

In my experience at the top of the mountain, you often encounter an underlying sense of sadness if you allow yourself to slow down. The reflection is too scary and the glare of the opportunity cost too bright. The relentless climb to the top becomes a solo journey—an unexpected necessity needed to lighten the load and climb faster. Until one day, you realize you feel completely alone even when surrounded by people who love you.

My advice is not to skip the climb, if that is what you are called and driven to do; just be sure your aims align with your why, so you chase a dream that is only yours to name.

**AWAKENING**

Overall, these shifts often come from deep personal introspection, personal development growth, and our evolution as humans. In the work I have done for this book, I will share many beautiful examples where the internal catalyst was a thirst for adventure, a spiritual awakening, a change due to life events, a relationship change, and exposure to a different culture.

No matter your Intensity Point, once you are there, you achieve new perspectives, you have more information, and you start to get curious about what comes next. You are awake and open to trying something new. Your reflection on what matters most has shifted and, in some cases, so have your values. You begin to take a life inventory yet find yourself uncertain of how to navigate the future, torn between the desire for change and the fear of the unknown.

It's time to question everything. What has served you in the past will not serve you now. Question your values and your vision for the future. At this point, you stop following the path that was woven for you by society. Here you realize life is short, and you need to carve your own way out to take control of writing your own story.

My hope is that by leaning into the Intensity Points that resonate most to you, I can help you to work through them in the coming chapters of this book. I coach many clients, in many industries, all working on different things.

The vast majority of my clients come to me during one or more Intensity Points looking for guidance. Time and time again when they are open and put in the work, the benefits they receive are immeasurable.

It is also pretty likely that more than one of these Intensity Points will resonate with you. But don't worry about that. I can help regardless of which one brought you here to my "doorstep."

In addition to these five key Intensity Points, so many other life experiences can be Intensity Points for us: mid-career changes, new locations, various life changes, and legacy careers as folks move into retirement.

The great news is that no matter how you got here, now that you know why and where here is, you have the power to spark what comes next and put the building blocks in place to live your most authentic life!

The SPARK Energy Transformation path awaits you, and your first step begins now. Mark "You Are Here" on your map, and together, let's embark on this journey to find a clearer path to your destination. Let's go!

## CHAPTER 2

# SPARK ENERGY TRANSFORMATION PROCESS

---

*"A mighty flame followeth a tiny spark."*

—DANTE ALIGHIERI

I was once called a firecracker, in what I suppose was an admiring way, by a highly regarded vice president at Google. He was a really buttoned-up corporate guy with great character but not the type to hand out those types of compliments. In that moment, it felt incredible to be seen, knowing he felt my Big Energy vibe even if he didn't completely understand it.

It only seems fitting that the process I have developed for life transformation is called the SPARK Energy Transformation Process. Because in the world of Big Energy, doesn't one little spark have the ability to lead to huge flames and fireworks?

The SPARK process has been a part of my life for quite some time now. I have used it personally to change and transform my own life over and over again. That's the beauty of this energy transformation work. It is not a one and done thing; it is a live ever-moving currency. It's about constantly developing and learning so you continue to explore, evolve, and harness your energy through multiple seasons of your life.

I feel so blessed that I get to share it with you right here, right now—because I promise you it is life altering.

Let me tell you the story of Sara, a woman who turned a vision into reality through determination and self-reflection. Sara had a goal: to become a top producer in her travel agency. But this wasn't just about hitting a number. It was about finding a deeper purpose. She envisioned herself at the top of the world, a manifestation of her potential, and used this image as the password to enter her new reality.

Sara's journey began by connecting the dots of her life. She started stepping into who she truly was, embracing her identity and allowing it to guide her forward. As she pursued her goal, she continually asked herself if this was truly her vision or just a bar set by someone else. After careful consideration, she realized that reaching this milestone would open doors for her future. It wasn't just about the recognition. It was about proving to herself that she could achieve something meaningful.

Her "why" wasn't driven by material desires; it was deeply personal. Sara had spent years caring for her family and aging parents, and now she wanted to do something for herself.

Achieving top producer status would mean financial success, yes, but also access to exclusive learning opportunities and the chance to connect with others who shared her passion.

Letting go of "shoulding" herself became a crucial part of her journey. With the support of counseling and a strong community, Sara learned to ask herself whether she was acting out of genuine desire or guilt and shame. This shift in mindset was a game-changer.

And then she did it. Sara became a top producer. But the real victory came next. She began to step into her true self, focusing more on group travel and creating life-changing experiences for others. A trip with her twin mom friends became a moment of fulfillment, both for her and for those she helped. Her love of travel connected with her story of being adopted, leading her to volunteer with a nonprofit supporting the adoption community. Sara found her passion in seeing women support each other, using travel as a means to do so.

Sara's journey shows that when you follow a process like the SPARK Energy Transformation Process, you can break free from the limiting beliefs, habits, and circumstances that hold you back. Just like Sara, you too can unlock your full potential and create a life that is not only successful but deeply meaningful. Together, we'll explore new opportunities, expand your horizons, and have a blast along the way.

So what is the SPARK Energy Transformation Process all about?

The SPARK process consists of five memorable steps: self-reflection, purpose, abandon, results, and kinetic energy. Our journey together isn't a rigid "how-to" plan but rather a choose-your-own-adventure. I'll share, and you can explore, numerous growth opportunities I have developed, researched, and experimented with, finding them effective. Remember, not everything will resonate with you, and that's perfectly okay! Think of it as a tasty new menu that you get to choose from.

My goal is to help you think differently, reflect more, and experiment with some new things.

This is a hands-on, interactive book, with each section offering prompts and exercises to help you thoroughly engage with the material. It can serve as either a standalone resource or a starting point for deeper work with me personally—through workshops, group sessions, or individual coaching. If you need additional resources to support you along the way, please feel free to reach out; I would love to hear from you.

Each of the five SPARK steps will be covered in a chapter of its own so you can explore each stage in the depth needed to undergo your transformation and engage in lasting change.

To start off, here is a quick peek at what each stage looks like so you have a clear understanding of what to expect and how they all work together. In the end, I promise to bring it all together in an authentic and sustainable way so no matter where you are in your life, you will be able to apply these exercises and the things you learn to either start new or get back on track.

**SELF-REFLECTION**

We begin this journey together by taking stock of where you are and where you have been. And through the power of self-reflection, you will question it all.

In this chapter, I will help you build a muscle around:

- Embracing silence to hear yourself.
- Listening for clarity.
- Disconnecting your personal identity from your work identity.
- Leveraging your decision-making skills to find solutions.
- Auditing sources that ignite and drain your energy.
- Conducting an annual practice of reviewing.

The goal of this chapter is all about reflecting and auditing your life to better understand where you are expending your energy versus where you'd like to be. By taking the time for self-reflection, you will begin to shine a light into the deepest corners of your life and soul, revealing all the treasures and the hidden truths waiting to be discovered before you start to dream big about what comes next.

**PURPOSE**

Your purpose gives your life meaning and direction; it is the driving force behind everything you do—the reason you get out of bed in the morning and the spark that ignites your passion. Purpose is the vision for your life. You could argue that this step is the most important one in the process. Admittedly, it took me a long time to develop because I wanted to include so much goodness but had limited space to share it all with you.

Without having clarity on what you want, you can become overwhelmed, stuck, or spinning in the minutiae of everyday life. In this chapter, we will spend time cultivating your sense of purpose, visualizing what the best version of your life looks like, and creating goals to get there.

When you know your purpose, everything just clicks into place, and you feel more fulfilled, more alive, and more—well, authentically you! Your purpose makes you unique and sets you apart from everyone else. It's like your personal mission statement—a roadmap to living your best life. And the best part is your purpose isn't set in stone. It's a journey, a constant exploration of who you are and what you're meant to do in this crazy, beautiful world. Because when you live with purpose, magic happens.

**ABANDON**

The abandon step is key to letting go of those energy drainers. In this chapter, we will work through unplugging, abandoning, and rewiring the drainers so we can focus on investing your energy currency where you need it most and where it lights you up. This is about letting go of old patterns and stories that are not serving you and overcoming obstacles that are in your way, keeping you from realizing your full potential.

I will walk you through abandoning: control issues, beating yourself up, fear that holds you back, and society's expectations. In addition, you explore the likelihood that you will, at some point, get derailed along the way and what to do when that happens, because change is hard, and it takes time to rewire for the future.

This chapter is all about dropping the unneeded baggage you are hauling with you into the next season. You will gain the power to choose what you leave behind, giving you that weightless feeling as you head into experimenting with new ideas and adventures. I will empower you to get rid of stuff that drains you because your energy is precious, and you deserve to invest in things that uplift and inspire you. Holding on to energy drainers can weigh you down, hinder your growth, and prevent you from living your best life.

By letting go of what no longer serves you, you create space for positivity, growth, and fulfillment to flourish. It's time to Marie Kondo your life and bid farewell to those energy drainers that have overstayed their welcome!

**RESULTS**

A fantastic concept, developed by the legendary leadership expert John C. Maxwell, is called the Law of the Rubber Band. The premise is that all living things grow and that growth requires stretching. Maxwell says, "Growth stops when you lose the tension of where you are and where you could be."[1]

Results are about focusing on what you need to put into place to achieve your goals and the impact you desire. Put simply, what steps do you need to take, what skills do you need to develop, and what actions do you need to implement to turn your dreams into goals, your goals into action, and ultimately achieve your personal success?

We cover the skills and training you might need, the habits to adopt, how to engage your support system, the importance of leveraging well-being for optimal results, the value of practicing through experiments, and how to ground yourself in gratitude. Oh, and there is some fun stuff in here about celebrating your wins and milestones along the way to keep you engaged, inspired, and moving forward each day.

Results matter because they're the yardstick indicating whether your efforts are paying off and you're making headway. Results also give you valuable feedback to adjust and improve your strategies along the way.

**KINETIC ENERGY**
Kinetic energy, in the context of this book, represents the dynamic force that propels you toward living your most authentic life by integrating your story, purpose, and actions into a cohesive narrative you own and can share.

By harnessing this energy, you'll unlock your authentic life, embracing vulnerability and articulating your story with clarity. Through concepts of authenticity, self-expression, values alignment, and crafting personal elevator pitches, you will transform your life and build genuine connections. Embracing and sharing your unique journey will unlock a happiness and fulfillment you never thought possible, allowing you to live more fully into your purpose.

Through this journey of self-discovery and acceptance, you will honor your truths without fear of judgment and start to peel back the veil of societal pressures and expectations. This will give you the ability to show up rooted in your radiance and Big Energy despite whatever room you are in, who you are with, or the topic at hand. This means showing up as your full unapologetic self, even in moments of uncertainty. Daring to be authentically you, I promise, will be the most empowering journey you'll ever embark on.

You are here and ready to get started. And guess what? This process is exactly what you need to move ahead from wherever you are at right now.

Martin Luther King Jr. introduced the idea of taking one step, even if you aren't able to see the entire stairway at the start of your journey. By embracing this perspective, we have a much greater capacity to accept failure and move on.[2] This process can be done at your own pace, without stress, and, although it does need to go in order, can be paced the way that best works for you.

So, let's move forward by giving yourself grace. From a place free of judgment, take step one: just turn the page.

## CHAPTER 3

# SELF-REFLECTION

---

*"Knowing yourself is the beginning of all wisdom."*
—ARISTOTLE

If you don't know where you are, how do you know where to go?

**SILENCE SPEAKS VOLUMES**

Reflection gives you the opportunity to see whether you have alignment and congruence between your actions and what you value, and it allows you to consider how you are prioritizing those values as a part of your everyday life.

Reflection sends back an image, light, or sound. If we apply this concept to our energy thread throughout this book, it's about playing back the moments, images, and movies in our heads that bring us the most energy rather than the ones that drag us down.

During the major Intensity Points of my own life, reflection was crucial in helping me recognize where I was out of sync, but the tools to get there simply were not available. Everything I found was forward-looking, and I was left wondering, How can we build a house if we don't have a blueprint for the foundation?

At the conclusion of my six-month mental health leave, I visited the award-winning Kripalu Center for Yoga & Health in the Berkshires mountains. Their core methodologies, including BRFWA (Breathe, Relax, Feel, Watch, Allow) along with an emphasis on compassion for oneself and others, provided me with exactly what I needed. Located in a former Jesuit monastery, Kripalu brought me an austerity and peacefulness that I had never experienced. It was ripe for reflection and rich in creative energy, nature, and yoga. I truly feel that the universe called me there, which was exactly where I was supposed to be.

Despite all of this, while there, my days started with an incredibly uncomfortable experience to me—the silent breakfast. Silent breakfasts, if you are not familiar, are exactly that. You eat your soul-nourishing food alongside all the other participants, never uttering a word. You grab your drinks, find your table, alone or with others, and enjoy your meal, completely silently.

I am deeply inquisitive and love hearing about people's lives and stories. So you can imagine that I also have big love for long and rambling conversations. To say I felt like a fish out of water would be putting it lightly. As a raging extrovert, I also don't really enjoy being alone, and I become especially agitated when I am alone with my own thoughts. I tend to overthink and ruminate, which begins to fuel the fire of stress within me.

But I digress. The intent of these reverent moments was to create a true connection to the earth, your food, and the space around you. They promoted mindfulness, intention, and openness to listening to your own inner dialogue before the day began. It is also said that "a meal taken in silence reduces stress, elevates immunity, and increases the body's ability to digest and fuel us for the day ahead."[1]

Initially, I avoided this retreat offering. Each breakfast I would find a place outside to eat, clear of the indoor silence. It was comfortable to be around the chatter and the noise, and I would often bring a good book or find a stranger to talk to. But each time I passed the silent room, I grew more curious.

Eventually, I made a new friend who participated daily. She was incredibly effervescent, full of energy, and shared my big extrovert energy, so I asked her what it was all about. Her answer stunned me.

"For years, I have used the reflection of others to guide where I should be going and what I should be doing, always comparing and looking for an answer. But when I relinquish myself to the silence, I am left only reflecting on what is inside me. I become the guide on my own path. A mirror unto myself, not others.

Her perception sounded so beautiful to me and opened me up to a curiosity of silence I never imagined possible. So I gave it a go. During the rest of my stay, I gradually grew accustomed to these quiet breakfasts, finding solace in my own thoughts and reflections.

As I tuned in more closely, I discovered a wealth of insights, reflections, and ideas. They flowed effortlessly out of me and onto the pages of my journal. The barriers of hurt, pain, and uncertainty began to crumble, revealing a remarkable sense of abundance and illuminating potential paths for my future. My self-critic had vanished, as had the opinions and ideas of others that I had held tightly for so many years.

During my final days, I used much of my time reflecting on my six months of leave as well as what I wanted for myself going forward. During this time I realized two of the things I wanted most were to be a great mom for my kids and to focus more seriously on my health.

I felt a sense of empowerment on my path while also grieving the fact that I knew corporate America was not going to offer me the opportunity to do either of those things. Once I accepted these truths, I was able to create a forward-looking life vision that protected what I valued most. I let go of the shame for wanting it, became aware of the obstacles that had knocked me down in the past, and stood confidently in my desires.

Overactivity hinders our ability to create space for reflection and to develop a forward-looking mission, and I certainly was guilty of that. This lack of reflection prevents us from gaining valuable insights, aligning with our goals, and creating a strategic vision for the future, ultimately impeding our growth.

Without silent reflection time, we are spinning in place, overwhelmed and unsure where to go. I always share a nature analogy here. In nature, if there is an empty patch of unfarmed land, it begins to fill with weeds—some may be beautiful, but none are intentional. Without a vision for our lives, we fill our time with the proverbial weeds of social media scrolling, numbing, and avoiding. Wouldn't we rather take the time to intentionally plant so we can harvest and nourish ourselves from the fruits of our labor?

> **Ignite the Spark:** So, my challenge to you is to try a silent breakfast at least once a week. Whether you are alone or with others, you are investing in yourself by actively listening to your thoughts.

**LISTENING BRINGS CLARITY**
The process to define clarity for your life begins with self-reflection. Investing in self-exploration and personal growth strategies aimed at understanding yourself better is key to helping you uncover your nonnegotiables and eventually your purpose.

Often this means healing emotional wounds and doing the tough work of accepting yourself despite your failures and flaws. It involves exploration into your own thoughts, emotions, beliefs, and behaviors and is a great way to uncover patterns to understand your own personal drivers.

Sometimes it is about breaking old habits and awakening yourself to what else can be possible.

When guiding my clients toward their goals, I always kick off by envisioning the end result, prompting them with the question, "What does success look like for you?" From there, I encourage them to articulate their aspirations in a positive, future-oriented manner, as if they already possess what they desire. For instance, rather than saying, "I am bad at communicating," we rephrase it to, "I am a confident and articulate communicator."

This approach taps into the incredible power of our brain's wiring. The science behind it is known as RAS (reticular activating system). It is evidence that focusing on the positive and repeatedly affirming our desires not only propels us into action but also enhances our capacity to overcome obstacles and achieve our goals. In essence, RAS is a scientifically grounded form of manifestation deeply rooted in the brain's neuroplasticity.[2]

This discovery of clarity through listening to yourself and reframing your thoughts from what you don't want to what you do want can be quite powerful. The more you reflect on who you want to be and start to say it out loud, the sooner you begin to believe it is true.

I like to call this type of work inner work. Inner work is all about what it sounds like—working from the inside out. Creating an awareness of what starts inside you and what you can control. Outside work, which we will get to later, is all about experiments and external levers, which are also important, but if we don't start from the inside out, we lose our ability to drive longevity and sustainability.

"The only thing I can do to get clarity is to get quiet." My friend Meg offers me that sage advice.

I have known Meg for well over a decade now, beginning in the early days when our girls cheered together and we were co-Girl Scout leaders. Our energies have always aligned, and we have certainly been through it all together.

Meg is an incredible inspiration and community to me, as she has experienced several Intensity Points in life that have rolled in like storms. She believes we spend our lives constantly "preparing our boats"—physically, spiritually, and emotionally—to withstand the storms of life. We must not only prepare our boats for these storms but also learn to enjoy the times when we are able to float in calm waters and enjoy the warmth of the sun.

Few people have the luxury of sailing calmly their entire life because storms will eventually brew—bringing a unique experience to all of us. Little did Meg know that the boat she had been building would offer her the anchor she needed for the storms awaiting her arrival.

Two of Meg's Intensity Points were profoundly tragic events that left indelible marks on her: rehabilitating her mom after a brain aneurysm and the devastating loss of her seven-year-old son, Porter.

It's been nearly three years since her family has lost Porter, and Meg says they are still trying to navigate the aftermath of the storm. Her inner knowing is the light guiding Meg and her family. Today, she realizes they have been her life boat as much as she has been theirs.

Meg continues on with courage and strength. She is—and will always be—one of the most inspirational and positive humans I know. She understands firsthand the power of stillness during Intensity Points, listening for the whispers of guidance that come with a sense of calm and soulful tranquility. This transcends the chaos of the physical world, allowing her the freedom to embrace the heartache she once ran from. She shared one of her favorite quotes from the Sufi mystic and poet, Jalāl al-Dīn Rūmī, "There is a voice that doesn't use words. Listen."[3]

Initially, she was introduced to this inner work practice through Transcendental Meditation (TM) developed by Maharishi Mahesh Yogi. TM is a silent meditation technique that involves sitting comfortably with your eyes closed and repeating a mantra in your head. The goal is to reach a state of restful alertness and transcend ordinary waking consciousness. Meg has honed her ability to find clarity through these meditation sessions.[4]

Although initially she set aside time and used TM a few times a day for twenty minutes, she can now effortlessly close her eyes anytime and access this state during brief moments of respite while waiting for her kids after practice or in the school pick-up line. She explained meditation does not have to be a formal process of complete silence of the mind but rather allowing those thoughts to float by like clouds and acknowledging them and letting them pass. Treat it like a muscle and practice it regularly, even in small doses, to eventually strengthen your inner resilience and clarity.

Meg shows us that the power of stillness is a fundamental aspect of personal growth. Listening to the voice within and her desire to keep Porter's love for others living on, she and her family founded the Porter Riedl Foundation. Because he selflessly gave immense kindness and generosity in his seven years, the foundation is continuing his tradition by and sharing this love with thousands of people. Most recently, the foundation secured more than five hundred donated bikes to provide kids the freedom to ride and feel the sun and wind on their faces.

Meg's story is one of transforming the hardest life moments into inspiration through deep reflection and reinventing her purpose on earth, showing us all that even after the toughest storms, we still have work to do. In her case, she is meant to be the light, the hope, and the inspiration to continue to give all the love you can, to all the people you can, even when your heart has been so hurt.

Charlie White, the inspiring 109-year-old man who lived through a century of upheaval, once said, "You cannot change what was, nor entirely control what will be. But you can choose who you are, what you stand for, and what you will try to accomplish."[5] This quote beautifully reflects her outlook on life.

**Ignite the Spark:** Want to try this listening to yourself thing out? A great way to do this is through having a clarifying conversation with yourself. Think of it as a private conversation with no reference to your external environment or importance of expectations. All you need is a semi-chill space where you can center yourself through some box breathing, a journal, and some uninterrupted time.

Start with box breathing—find a comfortable chair and sit with your feet on the floor. When you are ready, close your eyes and breathe in through your nose while counting slowly to four, focusing on feeling the air enter your lungs. Hold your breath while counting slowly to four and then slowly exhale for four seconds. Pause in between for a few seconds and then repeat a few times until you feel clear and calm. This is a great way to reset your breath and is incredibly useful to prepare you for clarity work and/or to reduce stress.

With your newfound calm, now take some time to ask yourself these questions:

- What is currently on my mind?
- What do I truly want in my personal and professional life?
- What dream am I holding myself back from?
- What is getting in my way?
- What is my mind/body/soul trying to tell me that I am not listening to?

> Let your thoughts and words flow naturally on the page as you imagine this conversation with your inner self. After writing for twenty or so minutes, review your notes and highlight what is most interesting to you.
>
> Summarize what you learned about yourself on a new page, and jot down any actionable steps that make sense for you. Regularly practicing this exercise will help you develop a deeper connection with your inner voice and gain greater clarity in your life.

I hope that was insightful and provided some clarity and self-reflection on where you are.

**YOUR WORK IS NOT YOUR IDENTITY**

What you do is not who you are.

Sorry, don't hate me, but it's true. Harold S. Kushner, American rabbi and author, said it right in my opinion, "Nobody on his deathbed ever said, 'I wish I had spent more time on my business.'"[6]

In *From Strength to Strength: Finding Success, Happiness, and Deep Purpose in the Second Half of Life,* Arthur C. Brooks expertly shows how we can use our past experiences to find deeper purpose and happiness after navigating Intensity Points and entering the second half of our lives.

He encourages us to pause and reflect on our experiences, integrating our past knowledge to promote personal growth. This approach helps prevent burnout and extends growth beyond mere professional achievements. In this work, we begin to recognize that our traditional work, role, or job does not define our identity, and we can build self-worth based on more intrinsic qualities and embrace a holistic self-concept. This approach leads to true fulfillment, better life balance, and sustainable success.[7]

As I stitch together his work with mine, I want to remind us to make sure we are invested in and highlighting our personal purpose and well-being equally, or above, how we have historically valued our professional accomplishments.

When I finally decided to leave my job at Google after thirteen years—the majority of my girls' lives—I was really scared to tell them. They loved Google. They had been to over a dozen Googleweens and take-your-child-to-work days, and they loved wearing all the cool Google/YouTube swag to school.

They bragged to teachers and friends about my success there. I was terrified they would see me as a failure for leaving such a prestigious career. Yet when I told them, "Mommy may not work at Google anymore," I was stunned by their reactions. My oldest, Grace, urged me to take the leap, believing I had so much to share in inspiring others to chase their dreams and embrace change.

My youngest Charlotte's reaction was also so enlightening as she thoughtfully paused and remarked, "Oh well, Mommy, if you don't work at Google, you will just do something else amazing—because you're amazing."

Such sage wisdom in their ten- and fifteen-year-old hearts.

And there it was. I was not Google. I was not defined by my role there. I was defined by my own merit of being successful, inside and outside those iconic primary-colored walls. I had put so much stock in the brand, confusing it for a family, which for many years it had been. It took me every bit of three months after leaving to detach myself from the big brand logo that had become deeply etched into my identity. It was like grieving a loss. Many times, I felt I was floating, having left my team, my family, and my role.

I now feel confident in telling people I am a retired Googler, a reformed ladder climber, and that I wouldn't change that for the world. I no longer begin my elevator pitch toting my Google stripes but instead lead with, "I help people transform and live the lives they never dreamed possible." Maybe not as highly traded on the stock market, but it feels dang amazing in my soul.

We all tend to do it, though. Our culture is deeply rooted in what we do, where we work, and what clubs we belong to. While it's neither right nor wrong, I now find it all a bit one-dimensional.

My friend Mic always begins a new conversation with the question, "What do you stand for or believe in?" which flips the script completely and is more rooted in how we are living our best life and what we value most as humans, versus what we do.

I recently met up with my previous boss at Google, Karen. We both left Google around the same time, and I had not seen her in about seven months. I knew she had recently graduated with her master's in organizational design, and I was curious to know what she was up to. As a fellow coach, I wanted to hear about her work and learn more about how launching her coaching business was going.

But when I asked how she was, she spent a good thirty minutes describing the "connection tour" she was on. She was focused on reconnecting with old friends, throughout the country, spending her time with family, and traveling to California with her husband to visit the people and places that mattered when they first began building their lives together.

Sharing the ways she was leaning into personal, creative, and collaborative projects, she never once mentioned her business until I asked. I was a bit taken aback. She had always valued family and friends, but given how much had changed professionally for both of us in the past year, I had anticipated her going there first.

But as she was talking, I thought I had never seen her so happy and full of joy.

Given how ingrained our day-to-day work becomes, we can often tell a story so associated with those details that we lose sight of portraying who we really are.

This is why I regularly focus on separating our unique qualities versus our work identity when I practice mock interviewing with my clients. We'll dive deeper into telling our origin stories and sharing our life experiences authentically and inspirationally in the "Kinetic Energy" chapter, so stay tuned.

For so many hours a day, we are defined by what we do and accomplish at work—measured all the while by our performance reviews—that when it comes time to remove that hat and "step outside those walls," we are unsure what to do.

We are not rewarded for joy and laughter, nor are we measured on minutes relaxed with a good book or watching a Disney movie with our kids. Doing versus being is rewarded. This leads to restlessness and unhappiness. Eventually we lose the capacity to find joy, and our enthusiasm for life disappears.

**Ignite the Spark:** I invite you to experiment a bit here by pausing to reflect on your attachment to your work identity. You can do this by taking inventory on how you define yourself at work as well as in all other roles in your life.

Take some time to reflect not only how and what this definition looks like but also the energy that you show up with in these roles. Explore work, roles as a mother, sister, daughter, friend—as well as other facets of your life like hobbies, relationships, and values.

Ask yourself, "How do I define myself in that space? What does my energy look like there? How attached am I to the story I am telling myself about myself in that role?"

I am excited to see what you learn!

**DECISION-MAKING SHAPES SOLUTIONS**

Okay, this one might seem a bit unconventional, but hear me out. Problem-solving and decision-making are fundamental skills that underpin much of what we do. They are versatile and adaptable, transferring with us across different goals and paths. By honing these skills, we can build robust frameworks for personal growth and effectively navigate various challenges.

The key here is to intentionally grow in your ability to navigate challenges, overcome obstacles, and have your own personal decision-making process. This will help you make progress toward your goals and help you in exploring different options, generating creative solutions, evaluating potential risks, and making informed decisions that align with your priorities and values.

When I personally made the move from big tech to coaching, I entertained three different paths through this exact process: staying at Google and securing a similar director-level role leading a large sales team, moving to another tech company, or the scariest, leaping off the corporate cliff and trying this scary thing called entrepreneurship.

As I looked at my paths and carved out the details of what I loved and what I was really good at, I started to uncover an important truth: the big team, big job with all the big pressure was no longer what I wanted at that moment. I also realized I didn't have to make a permanent decision right then. I just needed to make the next step, and a fresh change might be just what I needed.

Given this personal experience, paired with all of my coaching lessons, I am now quite adept at helping my clients decide between multiple options.

Olivia's story is one in which she was killin' it on her inner work. She had a regular cadence of meditation and reflection, had clearly outlined goals, and knew what she wanted in both her personal and professional life, yet she could not figure out what to do next. As she reviewed all her options, she felt overwhelmed, frustrated, and stuck.

When she came to me for help, she was trying to decide between three different options. She could stay in her corporate job in a financial firm and continue to strive for a promotion, which seemed to be taking forever. Or she could head out on her own to build a portfolio of businesses that included things she was passionate about, like writing the book she always dreamed about and flipping houses to create a passive income stream for her family. Lastly, she also contemplated leaving her firm of fifteen years to run a finance department at a smaller family-owned local company that would entail more scope, money, and expanded responsibility. She felt lost and was frankly embarrassed to have no idea which direction would suit her best after all these years. She was struggling and had lost faith in herself that her internal compass could lead the way.

So together, we tackled her problem one step at a time. First, we identified what the problem statement was (why she felt compelled for a change) and then we began problem-solving (creating decision trees, outlining her values, and essentially figuring out where we could experiment).

Since her inner work was in such a great place, we focused on her outer work—leveraging practical actions, strategies, tasks and setting up the challenge like a problem with multiple solutions. If you think about it like building a house, the inner work is the foundation (self-knowledge), and the outer work is like erecting the walls to that roof (goals) so you can arrive firmly and solidly on top.

> **Ignite the Spark:** The best way to do this is to audit those skills you already possess and are great at alongside what you are passionate about. Do this by drawing two overlapping circles on a piece of paper to make a Venn diagram.
>
> In one circle, you will conduct a skills assessment. Here, you will evaluate your current skills, knowledge, capabilities, and strengths.
>
> In the other circle, you will write what you know to be true about what energizes you. This could be working with people, analyzing data, or developing business.
>
> Lastly, you will look at the intersection of these things and jot them down in the middle. You are great at many things that don't energize you, and some things may energize you that you haven't really mastered the skills for yet. This exercise has been incredibly eye-opening for my clients, like Olivia, as they delve into what may be possible for them.
>
> Try it out yourself now!

As I shared, my personal passion has shifted from achievement to servitude during this second chapter of my career. This change came after leveraging the Venn diagram and problem-solving session myself. This newfound clarity gave me the confidence to leave the comfort of my current situation and make the move. Applying the same transferable problem-solving and decision-making skills that made me successful in the corporate world proved to be incredibly effective in this new context.

In the end, most people have some sort of tool or process they use in their everyday job that could be applied to practical decisions for their life. During a coaching engagement with my client Jo, I pointed this out, "Your superpower is creating and implementing strategic plans for a living. You have a process that you have used, which is celebrated for being comprehensive and impactful. What can you apply from that work to your own decision-making process of what comes next for you?" This was a total unlock for Jo, and we went on to do great work together that in the end led her to secure a role she loves.

**ENERGY ASSESSMENT FUELS POWER**

Next, let's assess our energy currency and where we are routing it. This involves a three-pronged approach—ignitors, drainers, and a yearly review.

At the root of the audit is understanding the answers to these questions: What brings you energy? What drags you down?

> **Ignite the Spark:** Grab a notebook or reach out to me for additional templates/exercises, and begin to reflect and collect your thoughts on the following.

**Ignitors:**

Things that bring you energy are those that really light you up. These could be events, connections, things you have read, things you learned, or even hobbies you have explored. These are usually rooted in fun and happiness. When you look at things that bring you energy, be on the hunt for healthy ways that you receive dopamine hits. What things that put you in a state of flow, leaving you wanting more anytime you're pulled away?

This is how I feel watching my three girls play soccer. During the entire game, I am all in but also wishing it would slow down and last longer. When the final whistle is blown, I am left wanting a new game to instantly begin. I have no worries or responsibilities. I am not obsessing over my to-do list or my inadequacies. I am just being and feeling. Just pure joy watching them play and compete. Because these precious moments ignite me in the way that they do, I am earnest in assuring I can make every game so as to not miss a moment.

These moments have also been profound in how I approach my coaching and training portfolio. I am thoughtful in reflecting on the clients I choose and assuring I am pursuing and then attracting work that ignites me and is aligned with my purpose.

Another illustration of an energy ignitor is when I interviewed Suzanne, a former partner in a top accounting and consulting firm, where she had little to no time to play. One year, she decided to handcraft all the Christmas gifts for her family. As a part of this journey, she ended up at a local Paint and Pour. If you are not familiar, this is the type of place where you join up with a group, have a cocktail, and collectively follow your instructor to complete a piece of art.

In completing a painting for her daughter, Suzanne found that she had entirely lost herself in the process of the art, in the journey of creation. She was reminded how much she loved the joy and freedom of creating something from a blank canvas and realized she was starving for more creativity in her overall life. This tiny spark began to ignite along with other nudges along the way and gave her the courage to move her family to Mexico for an adult gap year to explore what a new, more colorful creative world could look like for her. This adventure also led to launching her own business and publishing her first book *I'm Supposed to Be Doing This: An Adult Gap Year*, which is a must read!

**Drainers:**

Then there are energy drainers. Womp-womp.

These are the things that literally unplug you, leading to overwhelm and defeat. You wish you never had to do these things again, or you would immensely decrease. In these places you feel a deep state of incongruence between the life you want and the one you are actually living. Now sure, this may be something unavoidable, like laundry, but more likely these things are related to responsibilities. They can even be more nebulous things like gossiping, worrying, numbing, or ruminating in a shame that you have. They can be activities, but they may also be your feelings, so pay attention.

A few years ago, I launched a social program for our homeowners association. I secured a budget, developed their first ever full multiyear events plan, and set in motion to have four to six events per year. It was a ton of work, but it brought me a lot of joy. I pride myself in being in the business of "experience creation," so my heart was happy to see the joy in serving others. However, eventually, I was only getting the same three volunteers, my kids were no longer able to attend due to sports and school commitments, and my husband was becoming frustrated with the amount of work it took to host and clean up after the events. So this year when I did my energy assessment, I found it was no longer bringing me joy.

What had brought me such joy in year one was now draining me. I was "shoulding" in my head and ashamed over quitting. By engaging in these "I should" thoughts, I was effectively telling myself I would be failing if I walked away. But at the end of the day, and through reflection, I considered what I was missing out on because I was too proud to walk away.

Until finally I asked myself questions like: "What else could I be doing with that time that would bring me joy? What was the opportunity cost of leading in this role? Would I have more time with my family? Could I still leave my desired legacy of experience creation in other ways?"

Through this process, I arrived in a place where I was resolute in my decision to respectfully resign and to unplug from this once ignitor that had now become a drainer in order to rewire my currency to other spaces. Once I finally found the courage and said it out loud, I immediately felt a sense of lightness and relief, knowing I had made the right decision.

The power of reflection is that it helps you assess when and where these are showing up. Where are you? Who are you with? What are you doing? These things take a toll on your body too. They may be things that make your heart beat really fast, palms sweat, or tummy just feel nasty when you do them or potentially even think about them. Taking stock here really matters, because we do not have to settle for less. We don't have to do all the "shoulds."

> **Ignite the Spark:** My offering to you during this time of reflection is to start by getting every single one of these ignitors and drainers on paper and begin to think about where you want to say yes more often or no. And remember, everything comes with an opportunity cost.
>
> Listen to your body here. If you were to stop doing something that is draining you, what would that feel like in your body, your mind? Would it feel like regret? Relief? Unrest? If you were double down on one of your ignitors, what would that feel like?

## LOOKING IN THE REARVIEW MOVES YOU FORWARD
Lastly, after taking stock of your ignitors and drainers, review your past year. I call this "looking in the rearview mirror."

At this point, I want you to take stock of where you have focused over the past year.

Ask yourself, "What's the current state of my life?"

> **Ignite the Spark:** For this part of the process, pull out your planner, calendar, or vision boards to use in this annual reflection process. Give yourself at least an hour to go through this process.
>
> Audit how you spent your time over the past year. Review your activities and mark each one with a plus sign if it was an ignitor and a negative sign if it was a drainer.
>
> Once you have completed the exercise, you should have a pretty clear review of your own personal state of the union. We will use this as we enter into our "Purpose" and "Abandon" chapters as guiding lights when we get intentional on what we choose to unplug and/or rewire!

In the end, you can reflect a million different ways. The key is to prioritize it and be clear on what you do and do not want before moving to the next step.

In the upcoming chapters, you'll discover additional practices for reflection and awareness. Meanwhile, consider these key actions:

- Define what success means to you beyond your work role.
- Choose a reflection process that works for you and make it a priority.
- Assess what energizes and drains you.

- Apply your problem-solving skills to design your life.
- Pay attention to your body and soul as you shape your life.

Great work! And remember—if you don't know where you are, how do you know where to go?

# CHAPTER 4

# PUURPOSE

---

*"Make your vision so clear that your fears are irrelevant."*
—UNKNOWN

**CRAFTING THE LIFE YOU DESIRE**

Now that we have reflected on where we've been, it's time for the fun part—figuring out where you want to go!

Being open to possibilities is empowering and exciting, yet it can also be an overwhelming and daunting adventure. Opportunities, like Intensity Points, can arise unexpectedly, even when you thought the path ahead was smooth and well-planned.

This is exactly what happened to Amber.

Amber was a nurse during the pandemic. In the emergency room, she spent her days helping people navigate ailments while living in fear and isolation. Many of her patients were unfortunately on the cusp of life and death. More often than she wanted, she was put in a position to utter the words, "You might want to call your [closest family member]; this might be the last time you're able to talk to them before we put you on a ventilator." Years of experience had shaped her familiarity with life and death, but witnessing it at this pace suddenly made her acutely aware how precious time is and that our tomorrows are never guaranteed.

Amber's Intensity Point came one day when she suffered an emotional breakdown that left her sobbing in her car. It all rushed over her at once. She was lost, and time was ticking. She realized so many things in that moment, and for the first time in ages, she let it all go and immersed herself in her feelings.

The life she was leading, although she loved so many parts of it, was no longer in tune with who she was and aspired to be. Despite having a successful career and a home she loved, she found herself in a romantic relationship that was no longer fulfilling. Overall, she just felt like something was missing. To the outside world, her life seemed picture-perfect, but it didn't feel authentic. She no longer knew who she wanted to be or what she truly wanted in life.

What Amber did know was that it was time to explore the possibilities. It was time to try something different and explore herself, her wants, her passions, and, ultimately, the world.

For years, she'd had all kinds of professional goals, but now she knew it was time to pursue some personal goals. It was time to end the relationship that was no longer bringing her joy, take some much-needed vacation time off, and push the edges of her comfort zone.

One of her close friends and colleagues had recently quit their nursing job and relocated to Guatemala for a few months to escape the pressures of the pandemic. During Amber's initial conversation with her friend, she knew nothing about the country, but given her friend's love and energy for it, she trusted her gut. On a whim she booked a flight departing five days later.

During the month she spent in Guatemala, she indulged her curiosity by exploring a new culture and slowly began to discover what could be possible for herself. On paper, she seemed to have everything—degrees from prestigious schools, financial stability, valuable assets, and professional achievements. But as she met others who had what she might once have considered "nothing"—people who had quit their jobs to backpack around the world, work remotely, or embrace a slower pace of life—she realized they all shared something she deeply yearned for: happiness, contentment, and alignment in their new lives.

One of these strangers along the way quickly became a friend. He had left his job in the United States to open a small business in Guatemala selling blankets and giving back to the community. One day, he asked her a simple yet intense question: "What do you really want?"

She immediately launched into her rehearsed response of wanting to attend grad school, get married, and on— feeling very proud that she had a solid plan for the future.

He listened intently as she continued to recite her canned answers, and when she finally finished, he stared directly at her, challenging her: "Are you sure that's what you want?"

She was stunned. As she paused and saw the reflection of herself in his eyes, she realized she was missing the point. It all began to unravel in front of her. A nurse was what she did, not who she was; her things were what she owned, not what defined her. Real happiness for her, she realized, was exploring new experiences, habits for health, and relationships. Those things sparked her highest energy currency. From that moment on, she vowed to invest in what brought her joy, which was traveling and learning. From this vow came the goal to travel somewhere new each month over the course of the upcoming year. This goal was thrilling yet also overwhelming, but she was determined to listen to the universe and chase her dream.

That was four years ago, and since then she has visited more than twenty-two countries!

Each trip, whether her first or third, brings a unique experience. In Colombia, she witnessed an intense sense of family and mutual community support and was reminded how important these elements are to her. In Jordan, she learned about the importance of respecting different cultures and discovered how much she loved being curious and always learning. All of her experiences in other places gave her wisdom in connecting with others, slowing down, and really fine-tuning her definition of success.

She thrives on meeting new people, reconnecting with old friends, staying present, and celebrating diverse cultures. Focusing on personal growth, she tunes into her own preferences and surrounds herself with the right people. She nourishes her body, invests in restorative sleep, and embraces every moment with gratitude, finding renewed purpose and fulfillment. Above all, she cherishes the opportunity to try new things and wholeheartedly embraces travel as a way to receive all the world has to offer. The world is vast, and she's constantly eager for more.

She basically underwent a life-changing transformation, leading to more opportunity than she even thought possible.

Now, we can't all travel the world, and to some of you that may not even be attractive. But what if we went on a journey right here, in the safety of our own homes, through visualization?

**VISUALIZATION**
One of my favorite visualization exercises is something called hot pen.[1] I use it regularly with my clients in group coaching and during the transformational weekend workshops I run. The goal of this exercise is to visualize the best version of your life. Imagine a detailed snapshot of your future. What does your perfect life look like one year from now?

> **Ignite the Spark:** For this exercise, I will have you set a timer for twenty minutes, find a comfortable place, grab a few pieces of paper, and get ready to write. I want you to write down what you see for yourself one year from now if you were living your absolute best life. Be super

> specific. What would it look like if all your goals came true at the end of the year? For these precious twenty minutes, you are just going to keep writing, letting the story of your ideal life unfold, dreaming without editing and as if anything were possible.
>
> The only rules are that you cannot stop. Keep continuously writing regardless of what is showing up. This continuous writing will help you push through your thought barrier, self-consciousness, self-censorship, and self-doubt that inevitably sneak in when we start dreaming really freaking big. This continued writing will help those unguarded thoughts shine through and outpace your own natural self-editing. So try it out now!

How did it go? I am hoping this exercise provided you with much-needed expansiveness and abundance. I once had a vision workshop attendee who was resistant to the exercise, but once she completed it, she told me, "That was incredibly eye-opening. I went in thinking my life was already fantastic, with nothing more to want, but I came out overflowing with new, inspiring dreams I never even allowed myself to consider!"

This is a great exercise for both your personal and professional life. In addition, I have also leveraged it with leaders as they shape what they want the vision of their team to look like. In any instance, the goal is the same: to allow yourself to live in a world of "what if" and "what could be!"

Next, take a few minutes to reflect on the why. Why are the dreams that came to you during this exercise so important?

What really lit you up? What surprised you? What is missing from the picture you painted, and what does that tell you? Just spend some time reflecting on what came up. Don't get into the how yet. Just get curious about what poured out of you.

## VALUES AND PRIORITIES

A powerful way to bring clarity and create a well-rounded, fulfilling life is to begin by identifying your core values and priorities.

> **Ignite the Spark:** This journey starts by exploring a comprehensive list of values. There are plenty offered online, and I recommend you find the largest list you can (one hundred values is great).
>
> Once you have the list, use your gut to circle the top ten that resonate most with you. Don't overthink it. Just choose those that speak to you. Once you have completed that, go back and highlight the top three that seem most critical for your life. This sounds simple but is actually a pretty difficult thing to do for most people. Just follow your gut and remember there are no right or wrong answers. When you have these top three values, you can use them to filter the decisions you make and where you direct your energy in life.

Mike is a great example of living a life rooted deeply in his values. Immigrating from Poland at the age of seventeen, Mike identifies "support" as one of his key values. As such, he has made it his life's work to support people who need it most—both in plain sight and behind the scenes. He holds this value dearly because of the support he received while establishing himself in the United States. Mike pours himself into this work through time, energy, and financial assistance.

As a successful former tech executive, he could easily leverage his resources to collect expensive material things, yet he is so deeply rooted in his values that he spent last year focused on personally crowdfunding five thousand soccer balls and traveling to the Ukraine to personally deliver them to children. In knowing his core values, he can identify what personal success looks like for him, and the payoff is incredible.

Values help you understand what to prioritize and where to focus your precious energy. As entrepreneur, author, and motivational speaker, Jim Rohn says, "If it is a priority, you will find a way, if it is not, you will find an excuse." Rohn's quote underscores the importance of aligning our commitments and intentions with what truly matters. He challenges us to reflect on our true priorities and ensure our actions align with our goals and values.[2]

The wheel of life exercise is the best tool I have found for getting your priorities in order. It consists of a circular diagram divided into six or eight sections, each representing a different aspect or dimension of your life. I call each of these dimensions your key priorities. Some of the top categories people choose are: career, finances, health, family, personal development, community, spirituality, self-care, fun, adventure, and mental health.[3]

Start by plotting out six to eight priorities that resonate with you, assigning each of them a slice of the pie. Depending on where you are in a particular season, or year, this may look differently. I recommend that you reevaluate annually—just as you do your overall vision and life alignment process to allow for evolution and fine-tuning.

The purpose of this exercise is to provide a holistic view of your life and highlight areas where you may need more focus or energy redirection. It helps you align your values and priorities and serve as a foundation for setting goals and creating action plans.

Once you have your wheel completed, let's choose a few rituals for each priority. These rituals are one or two actions that you can start with to move you toward priority alignment and achieving your goals.

For example, if I have health as my priority, the rituals that will help me achieve it may be 1) Sunday meal planning and 2) calendaring my workouts.

These rituals will help assure your momentum and help you to measure milestones along the way. Remember, motivation does not happen on its own. Focusing on positive momentum is the key. The more momentum you gain by performing these rituals time and again and begin to see the results you desire, the more motivated you become to continue. Designing your life to create space for these rituals is the next best step to spark your momentum. We will talk more about logistics and tactics on this later in the book.

## MANIFESTING THROUGH VISION BOARDS

The next step in my process is to create a tangible version of your life vision. You can do this a few ways, but my favorite way is by creating a vision board.

These activities are often most effective when done within a community. Since you're here with me reading this book, I'll give you an overview of why they work, what they involve, and how they're essential for reaching your personal development goals. Then you can complete one on your own.

Essentially, your vision board is a collage of your deepest desires and a sneak peek into the future you desire!

It is a way to stimulate your creative energy and design a visual that showcases your dreams and goals through pictures, quotes, and words. It's putting your aspirations front and center, reminding you daily of where you want to go and manifesting what you want. Whether it's traveling the world, landing that dream job, or finding inner peace, a vision board has your back.

Your board will become a visual representation of a well-rounded version of your life. When you dig in, be sure to bring in those foundational items we just reviewed (visualization, values, priorities, and so on) and search for both pictures and words to symbolize that new version of you.

I have been leveraging vision boards for more than a decade to help myself and my community create breathing space and energy around goals. In creating your board and putting your vision into the universe, you also set yourself up for manifestation and the law of attraction—meaning that when you call your shot, your thoughts and beliefs will influence the outcomes you are looking for.

Crafting and displaying your vision board somewhere you will see it regularly and reflecting on it will not only remind you of where you are going but create powerful positive affirmations and images that align your subconscious mind with your conscious goals and intentions. Ultimately, you will facilitate the process of manifesting your dreams, turning them into realities.

I get so pumped when I see this in action! Here are a few snippets from past workshops where participants shared their dreams coming true.

Jodi shared: "Our family has been planning a trip to England since 2020, and due to things out of our control, we didn't make it. This year, I almost didn't put it on my vision board for fear it wouldn't happen, but I am so glad I did! We are planning our trip for June 2023!"

Angie shared: "Putting big goals on my vision board made me more accountable and focused. Feeling inspired, I intentionally planned how to achieve them, and when I achieved one of my goals, I felt a much greater sense of accomplishment. I won a trip to Hawaii in May and am committed to my weekly yoga and fitness goals!"

In addition, when faced with challenges or setbacks, revisiting your vision board can reignite your motivation and enthusiasm, reminding you of all the reasons you started chasing your dreams in the first place.

Here are a few stories of how vision boards have changed my life.

The first was my 2022 board. In the middle of my board that year, I had pasted the word "retire" in big huge bold blue type, meaning that I wanted to begin thinking about how I would exit corporate America in the next seven years, when my youngest finally left the nest. At that point, my husband and I would be fifty-six years old. Day after day, I would revisit my board, displayed on my office wall, and strategize how to make it happen. I was very intentional on continuing to build and put one foot in front of the other, despite the incredibly difficult season I was in.

This was around the time I entered the life crisis I described in this book's Introduction. By the time I was navigating my three swim lanes in late 2022, it finally hit me what my board was trying to tell me—what I had manifested without even knowing it. I would retire from Google now. What was I waiting for? I had all the blocks in place, and retiring did not have to mean forever, but retiring from Google was the next best step for me. Leaning into my retirement plan, and second-chapter career, a good seven years early felt amazing and was exactly what was meant to happen. The universe knew.

In 2023, I was toying with a way to take my family on an epic adventure. We had tried for three years to travel somewhere tropical, but it was just not in the cards. On a dark and gloomy

February day, my daughter Madeline and I were walking the dog together and commiserating about how badly we needed a change of pace, the sun, and the tropics to soothe our souls. Forty minutes later, we decided we were going to make it happen. We were going to move somewhere for an entire month. Only when we got back home did we realize it was February 2, Groundhog Day—it's meaning definitely not lost on us.

*What about Costa Rica?* I pondered. I had always been curious about a country known for its culture of generous and joyful people, mountains, waterfalls, rainforests, and oceans. Two days later, the deal was sealed when I kicked off my vision board event. During my event kick-off, I picked up a bunch of bananas to use as a metaphor for nurturing growth, and I was stunned to see six perfect stickers staring back at me: "A Product of Costa Rica." No way was this not going on my board! In July of 2023, the Kulongowski crew set off to live in a treehouse villa full of monkeys, macaws, lizards, sloths, and even scorpions—in the middle of a Costa Rican rainforest.

I firmly believe that without my intentionality and the visual manifestation of my vision boards, my dreams would not have come to life. If I hadn't allowed myself to dream big and challenge conventional paths, I would still be stuck in a stressful job, counting the days until retirement. I might have enjoyed a beautiful summer on the lake in Michigan, but I wouldn't have experienced the deep connections and growth that came from facing challenges in Costa Rica with my family. My vision board became more than a collage of aspirations; it was a testament to my willingness to explore the unknown and defy the status quo.

So even if you do not identify as "being creative," I encourage you to try something different and step into uncharted territory with the hope of discovering something new and maybe even hidden within yourself! Letting yourself explore this creativity enables alternative ways of seeing the world. It unblocks old patterns or habits and allows for nonlinear thinking.

In writing *The Gifts of Imperfection,* Brené Brown learned and shared a lot about creativity. She says, "People who say, 'I'm not very creative' doesn't work. There's no such thing as creative people and non creative people. There are only people who use their creativity and people who don't. Unused creativity isn't benign. It lives within us until it's expressed, neglected to death, or suffocated by resentment and fear. If we don't use our creativity, it metastasizes into resentment, grief, and heartbreak. People sit on that creativity or they deny it and it festers. The only unique contribution that we will ever make in this world will be born of our creativity."[4]

In this journey of self-discovery and personal growth, we need to trust ourselves and have the courage to try something new that propels us forward, igniting the spark of possibility and leading us to unforeseen heights.

> **Ignite the Spark:** Dare to pick up those scissors, flip through those magazines, and craft a vision board that reflects the boundless potential within you. After all,

> the greatest adventures often begin with a single step outside the familiar.

Now that we have visualized our best life, identified our values and priorities, and have a beautiful visual manifestation to remind us daily where we are headed, let's make it actionable!

## GOALS

"I thought I needed help building habits, and that work was really helpful, but getting to my 'why' helped me exponentially to unlock what I needed," Stephanie mentioned to me during one of our sessions. "You really helped me to reframe how I thought about self-development and guided me to dedicate time daily to take care of myself and unlock what the next version of me could be."

Five years ago, Stephanie became one of my clients through a women's advancement program where I volunteered as a coach. Since then, she has remained a steadfast client. Initially, her focus was on establishing habits for long-term progress. However, we quickly discovered that understanding her why was fundamental to developing her goals, and eventually the habits would follow.

Reframing her bigger why and overall goals inspired her to develop new habits, commit to them, and stay true to herself. As we implemented her plan and habits together, beautiful things unfolded for her. She was promoted at work and reached her peak fitness. Most importantly, she was the happiest she had been in a very long time. Now years later, we are still able to leverage that foundation, her why, her key goals, and her habits to stack goodness upon goodness, leading to her continued personal and professional success.

Setting goals and focusing on your results in an intentional way is crucial for personal and professional development. There are so many reasons that goals are important to achieving our overall dreams and the life we want. But most importantly, they give us direction, purpose, and a drive for achievement. They also create a sense of urgency and inspiration, helping us attain measurable progress and accountability. Overall, this contributes significantly to your success and well-being.

Earlier, we talked about the wheel of life, where you align your life's vision with your priorities to ensure they are congruent with your values. If you think of it as a funnel, it goes: vision, values, priorities, goals, and then habits. But before we celebrate and measure that success, let's talk a bit about laying out those goals and how we make the most of doing that.

SMART goals are a framework for setting clear and achievable objectives. The acronym SMART, as developed by George T. Doran in 1981, stands for specific, measurable, achievable, relevant, and time-bound.[5]

Goals should be specific in that they are clear and well-defined, answering the questions of who, what, when, where, and why. This provides a precise direction for action. They should also be quantifiable, so we can track and assess our progress. Measurable goals also help us determine when you have achieved them, or how close you are. They should be at the edge of your learning curve but at the same time achievable in that they are realistic and attainable, considering the resources, skills, and time available to you. In short, they should stretch you just beyond your comfort zone but remain within the realm of possibility.

Let's use an example of losing weight. I have broken it out by each dimension below and then simplified it into one comprehensive SMART goal.

**Specific:** I want to lose ten pounds.

**Measurable:** I will track my weight loss progress by weighing myself once a week.

**Achievable:** I will achieve this by maintaining a calorie deficit of five hundred calories per day, exercising for at least thirty minutes five times a week, and drinking eight glasses of water a day.

**Relevant:** Losing ten pounds will help improve my overall health, increase my energy levels, and boost my self-confidence.

**Time-bound:** I will achieve this goal within three months.

**SMART Goal:** I will lose ten pounds within three months by maintaining a calorie deficit of five hundred calories per day, exercising for at least thirty minutes five times a week, and drinking eight glasses of water a day. I will track my progress by checking my daily wins and weighing myself once a week.

The best way to increase your ability to achieve your SMART goals and prove intentionality to yourself is by integrating the practice of writing down your goals. This will help you find a clear roadmap to follow for success while ensuring that your objectives are specific, measurable, achievable, relevant, and time-bound.

Studies show that you are 42 percent more likely to achieve your goals if you write them down. Documenting your goals, intentions, and priorities enhances clarity and focus. Additionally, research indicates that you are 76 percent more likely to succeed if you capture actions and commitments while tracking your progress on a weekly basis.[6]

> **Ignite the Spark:** So let's try this out. Practice carving out a few SMART goals to get that momentum going!

**CHOOSE YOUR BOULDER**

That was a lot to take in—so much dreaming and goal-setting! But by the end of the day, this process will bring focus and clarity if we begin by prioritizing one major goal to start with. Authors Gary W. Keller (founder of Keller Williams Real Estate) and Jay Papasan (VP of Strategic Content, Keller Williams) share great insights in the book *The ONE thing*. "Until my one thing is done—everything else is a distraction."[7] So I always encourage my clients to prioritize their most significant and impactful goal first, one that will lead to exponential success across all that they do if they unlock it.

Here is a perfect analogy: If you throw a handful of pebbles into a lake, they will make tiny splashes. However, if you drop one large boulder in, it will create a huge splash and amplify through an amazing ripple effect. So if you think about all of your goals and your big why, what's the one thing you can start with that will create a flywheel and become a catalyst for all of your other goals to fall into place? This is where you will start your journey. If you work to master that one thing, that boulder, all of your other successes will continue to blossom as well.

In my forties, I was laser focused on my boulder—getting back into the best shape of my life through focusing on my health. As a result, I was the happiest I had ever been in my adult life and in the best physical shape since my teenage athlete years.

I set the goal a year in advance in preparation of a cruise for my brother's fortieth to the Bahamas and Cuba.

It all started with my why, which was pretty big for me—to prove to myself that it was possible, that I was worth it. To prove I was not halfway through this life but still had more than halfway yet to go. I could be strong again and show myself and my kids that with hard work and dedication, you can have what you want. With that big why, I identified my values, created my vision, outlined my SMART goals, and put in place some pretty legit habits.

To fuel my energy, I concentrated on filling up my cup with inspirational and motivational books, podcasts, events, and more.

I kicked off with my favorite motivational speaker, Rachel Hollis, by joining her Last 90 Days program at the end of 2018. The Last 90 Days is all about treating the last three months of the year as if they were the first three months of the year. Instead of self-sabotaging through the holidays, you are part of an online intentional community that is ramping up in October to prepare for an even more amazing start of the following new year.

In doing this, I adopted a morning routine that included many new healthy habits that gave me all the energy and tools to keep me excited and motivated. Tactically, it included going to bed early; making my coffee the night before; laying out my workout clothes; and getting up much earlier to invest in personal development, create content, get my workout in, and meditate to start my day.[8]

At first, the early morning part sucked, but in time I became so excited about what I "got" to do each morning that I would be pumped to go to bed early thinking about my coffee and personal development books. Transformation of the mind took about two weeks. Transformation of the body—if I remember right—took a lagging two months, but soon I turned a corner. What did this process require? I had to be patient; I had to put all my energy into my why but allow myself to enjoy the journey. I also had to allow for the hard parts as well as the fun parts, and I had to give myself grace where I needed it.

But most of all, I did not stop because achieving this boulder was helping so many pieces of my life fall into place. My momentum was turning into motivation.

If I didn't feel up to it, I did it anyway. If I was tired, I did it anyway. No matter what, I would put one foot in front of the other—making healthy meals, getting on the darn treadmill, sleeping my eight hours—and build success on top of success, never letting myself down. On top of wearing the bikini, getting promoted, launching my side hustle, and being incredibly "in it" with my kids, what I take away from my era of focusing on my one big boulder is I had never been so proud of myself. And that was worth everything!

I think we all know setting goals is an essential aspect of personal and professional development, but that is only half of it. To actually make it happen, as you can see in my example, we need strong habits and rituals to chip away at our goals step by step. In fact, goals and habits are two sides of the success coin, and without effective habits, we will lack the mental discipline to achieve our goals—no matter how much we want them. I will share more about habit creation in the Results step.

**MIND MAPPING**
Let's explore mind mapping, also known as "radiant thinking," which is a visual technique that enhances your thinking and helps you craft your purpose and life design. By organizing your dreams, goals, ideas, and passions in an interconnected manner, mind mapping enables you to brainstorm and see the relationships between your various pursuits. This process provides clarity, focus, and direction, allowing you to explore options, gain insight, and take meaningful action toward a life that aligns with your passions and values.[9]

> **Ignite the Spark:** For this exercise, let's start with what your big "why" is. At its core, a mind map starts with a central idea. You can do this by using a provocative question like, "What is the legacy I want to leave?" or "What brings me the most passion?" or "What do I want my life to look like this year?"
>
> From there, start by adding in related ideas or subtopics that branch out from the central node. In circles around these ideas or subtopics, write the first things that flow in your mind. These will be anything related to your central circle or to the other subtopics that branch out from the center.

I usually do three or four of these at the start of a new year. This year, I had a mind map with a center that said, "Help transform the lives of 240 people." I was on this "twenty-four for 2024" kick all around with twenty-four workouts a month and such. Coming out of that center, I began to build a web that had coaching, speaking, podcasts, social media content, finishing this book, building workshops, and so on. These types of things would help empower that inner goal and make it come to life.

Then, out of each of those circles, I added more to my web in terms of what would need to be true for all of these things to happen. What skills, learning, tools, and resources would I need to make it all possible? So for my example, I had things like: find a publisher, learn how to host a podcast, and take social media courses to help connect with new coaching clients.

In doing this, your web begins to form associations and interconnections that come together and provide you with tangible actions to chip away at your goals.

Congratulations on discovering your purpose!

This journey is not only a way for us to find the answers to what we want but also to embrace the questions that lead us closer to understanding ourselves and our place in the world. Think of your purpose like the flashlight illuminating the path ahead. Your purpose is not just a destination; it's the journey you embark on each day, shaping the legacy you want to leave behind and enabling you to live the best version of your life possible. You must create a vision for your life that is life giving and inspiring.

As we move forward, I invite you to ask yourself a few important questions. What would life look like if you had the courage to fully embrace the vision you've created for yourself, even if parts of it feel unconventional? What if you lived free from the constraints of societal expectations and the constant pressure of all the "shoulds"?

Now, imagine what it would mean to live a life so deeply filled with purpose that each day brings excitement. How would it feel to wake up eager to see this vision unfold before you?

In the end, embrace your journey toward purpose with courage and clarity, for when you find your purpose, you ignite not only a light that guides you but also illuminate the way for others.

# CHAPTER 5

# ABANDON (AND UNPLUG)

---

*"We must let go of the life we have planned, so as to accept the one that is waiting for us."*

—JOSEPH CAMPBELL

Let me tell you about Dave. Dave and I go way back to early Google days when we shared an office and a sales team. I am blessed to say I had an incredible amount of learning and laughs with Dave throughout the years. I feel so lucky to call him a friend because he is not only a great leader but one of the most authentic and kind humans I've ever met.

One of Dave's most significant Intensity Points came through surviving a near-death experience. However, given Dave's view, he saw the experience as an opportunity to improve and grow.

The near-death experience came when he recently ran his first full-distance Ironman. He coveted the dream of completing an Ironman race for years. In the end, though, despite training for over a year, he was ultimately unable to complete it.

He said, "I felt like a failure. Success would have required me to run another 6.8 miles. On any other day, I would have been thrilled to achieve what I did. I swam, biked, and ran more miles collectively than I had ever done before. But that was not my goal. My goal was to complete the Ironman, not just compete in it."

So what happened? Dave was incredibly fit, and as I mentioned, he rigorously trained and challenged his body to swim, bike, and run for over a year. Yet near the end of the run, he knew something was very wrong and was forced by his body to stop. Despite his intense training, the extreme heat of the day had depleted his electrolytes, and his body was not absorbing the nutrients.

At risk of cardiac arrest, with disturbingly low potassium levels, he ended up in the emergency room less than thirty minutes after the race. A team of doctors and nurses pumped him full of electrolytes, and he left fifteen hours later good as new. Although he didn't leave with a finisher medal, he came away with something much more powerful—perspective.

He had not failed. He had completed 95 percent of the race. It took him some time to get there, working through the disappointment and frustration, but he realized he had to stop being hypercritical of his performance. We don't always need to hit that 100 percent, perfect A+ score to be worthy and accomplished. Achieving something as great as 95 percent was pretty damn epic, covering more miles of land and sea than he ever had before. In fact, with only 1.36 million of the world's 7.9 billion population competing triathlon races per year (0.0172 percent), I'd say his showing was unbelievably impressive.[1]

As Dave and I continued to talk about his letting go of that perfection and self-critical mindset, his story transcended into a conversation on "Micro Intensity Points"—moments that have redirected his focus and guided him along his journey over and over again.

Similar to his Ironman journey, Dave emphasizes the importance of learning, recalibrating, and adapting as these Intensity Points gradually shape our trajectory. He and I agreed that they serve as guides, enabling adjustments as we navigate life's path, thus preventing energy crisis. It is also important to practice self-awareness and filter our next steps based on one's body and energy signals, and be flexible in response to changing circumstances.

By continually aligning with our energy, we eventually reach a point of affirmation, facilitated by self-awareness and presence in the moment. This practice of making these incremental moves and stacking our lessons learned fosters growth.

Dave's story shines a light on the fact that we should abandon things that are not serving us, which in his case was letting go of perfectionism. In doing this, he was then able to open up a whole new world. By letting go and unplugging these old thoughts, like Dave did with perfectionism, we can refine our focus and tap into where positive energy truly resides.

So spoiler alert, that is what this chapter is all about: abandoning and unplugging our energy drainers and rewiring ourselves in order to fuel our best energy currency.

## ABANDON (AND UNPLUG): CONTROL

I first met Cheryl through the annual pink out football game. Both of our daughters were on our hometown varsity cheer team, and each year, breast cancer survivors were asked to walk onto the field and bask in the love and support of the community. It was an opportunity to commend them on their bravery and resilience in the fight against a very brutal disease.

As the cheer mom and survivor pink out chair, I led the annual event to celebrate survivors, and Cheryl reached out to participate. I instantly loved her energy and serendipitously continued to run into her at events and engagements thereafter. I knew this was no coincidence, and each time we connected, I learned so much from her. She had such wisdom to share on bravery, letting go of a need to control, and the power of remaining positive despite all odds.

In 2019, Cheryl had pushed through and survived an entire year of her cancer journey. She experienced the life-changing event of ringing the final cancer treatment bell at the beginning of 2020 and, as an author, was at the precipice of publishing and launching her first book, *The Other Side of Sanctuary*.[2]

On the other side of her Intensity point, having battled and grown through her journey, she could see the light at the end of the tunnel. Momentum for her book began to heat up, and finally in January 2020 it was published. Life was good.

Early in March of 2020, she had finally reached a life-time dream and milestone. Her first book reading was scheduled at Pages Bookshop in Detroit. She was more ready than she had ever been to launch and was overcome with feelings of excitement and gratitude. But on the eve of the event, she received a text informing her the event was canceled. Something called COVID-19 was threatening the health of the community of Detroit and, possibly even more dramatically, the world.

Cheryl was in a state of disbelief, stunned and shaken to the core. How could this be? She had spent an entire year at home already—away from her community to heal and conquer cancer. She wanted to be back in the world. To say that she was crushed was an understatement. She had seen her ticket into a bright new life with a fresh restart, achieving something she had dreamed for years finally becoming possible. And it was over before it began. Trapped again at home, isolated and without control over her destiny, Cheryl looked inward. She knew there had to be a lesson and a chance for personal growth. She was much too reflective to let this lesson go unlearned, so she leaned into meditation and journaling to work through it.

It did not happen overnight, but Cheryl began to slowly accept her lack of control. She found peace in knowing that not everything is in our ability to make happen and began to more fully focus on embracing the present moment as it is. Instead of being angry and worrying about outcomes beyond her control, she was able to concentrate on her actions, attitude, and responses.

She had learned from cancer to take things as they came. She had struggled with control over her life, her family, and her career, and cancer certainly felt like a complete loss of control. One of the most profound things she said to me during our interview was: "I had a fear that I might lose everything then, and I wasn't even sure what everything was." I could feel her so deeply in that moment. By letting go of the need for control, she was finally able to overcome her fear of loss and find a path forward.

In a world where we spend our life planning it all out to run smoothly and move forward, setbacks and loss of control are devastating to us.

**REWIRE CONTROL: ACCEPT AND TRUST**
Cheryl's story illustrates that personal growth and letting go of the need to control all aspects of life take time. Experimenting with different approaches can help you move toward a more flexible and adaptive mindset while cultivating an attitude that embraces change and uncertainty as natural parts of your journey. Practices such as mindfulness, meditation, deep breathing, and yoga can enhance your awareness of thoughts and emotions without judgment. Accept that you

can't control everything and learn to embrace the present moment as it is.

In addition, delegating tasks and trusting others can significantly ease your burden, allowing you to focus on what truly matters. Recognize that you don't have to handle everything alone; collaboration and teamwork can be incredibly valuable. Shift your focus from controlling external circumstances to concentrating on what you can influence, fostering a healthier approach to managing your life.

> **Ignite the Spark:** Want to experiment with letting go? Sometimes using something to release and symbolize letting go of control can be really helpful. For instance, write down one or two specific things you're trying to control on separate pieces of paper. Light a candle, and one by one, safely burn these papers. You can also put them away in a symbolic container, or shred them and toss them in the trash. As you do, visualize releasing these concerns and letting them float away. This ritual is a great way to acknowledge the process of surrendering control and encourages a sense of peace and acceptance.

### ABANDON (AND UNPLUG): SELF-BLAME

I didn't fully grasp the impact of self-criticism until I experienced its release. During a sound healing session, I let go of the self-anger and resentment I'd been holding on to, which was life-altering. At that point, I finally came to terms with the deep anger and self-disgust I had been unknowingly carrying for so long.

During the sound bath session, the practitioner asked us to take a card from her hand without looking at it. She explained that the card we had chosen would undoubtedly "speak" to us in some way and help us to set our intentions for the experience.

When I turned my card over I had: "Self-forgiveness: Let go of old guilt and remember that you're God's perfect child." I was mildly curious but had no idea what was to come for me. The music began, the instructor walked the floor, the bowls began ringing, and the beautiful inspirational incense filled the room. If I am honest, as a first timer, it all felt a little hokey.

Finally, it was my turn, and although my eyes had been closed for the better part of twenty minutes, I could sense the practitioner's presence above me. As she rang my bowl, without warning, my eyes immediately began watering. The nurturing attention and sound connection created a profound surge of universal love within me.

The tears poured, and I begged for the moment to never end. It was one of the most powerful experiences I had ever felt, and I just wanted to bask in the attention and energy. Then something wild happened. At the site of my breast cancer surgery scar on my left breast, warmth slowly began to radiate—as if a stove burner was heating up. It became steadily more intense until eventually it felt like my breast and left arm were on fire. However, despite the heat, I didn't feel afraid or sense the pain; instead of burning me, I knew in that moment the heat was healing me. In that moment, all of my fear, anger, and hurt exited my body and began to vaporize into the air around me.

I felt this incredible sadness followed by a relief of forgiveness. It was self-forgiveness: forgiveness to my body for its weakness, for failing me and leaving me open to the sickness of cancer; forgiveness to myself for my perceived failing at my job and letting my family down with my declining physical and mental health; and finally forgiving the universe for putting me through it all.

In that moment, I felt all of my anger and shame burn away into the ether. I hadn't realized the stronghold these negative voices had on me and the lengths they were holding me back until that moment. I was ready to break free and embrace a new narrative that empowered me to recognize my worth and potential.

**REWIRE SELF-BLAME: SELF-COMPASSION**
One of the greatest gifts we can give ourselves is the empathy and forgiveness needed to face life's disappointments, failures, and flaws. This self-compassion fosters the bravery and confidence we need to move forward.

Embracing our flaws and vulnerabilities with gentle kindness helps us to nurture the seeds of resilience and unlock our boundless potential. Self-compassion isn't just an act of grace; it's a declaration of love and understanding that paves the way for growth and empowerment.

Without it, we become stuck and frustrated because, let's be real, we can all sometimes be pretty mean to ourselves. Can you imagine any successful person achieving what they have if their best friend was constantly chirping in their ear, "You are not good enough, you have failed, why even bother," all the time? So why do we do it to ourselves?

Too often, we allow the self-critic, or saboteur, to rule the roost and tell us what we are not capable of before we are even able to start. I recently had the opportunity to attend a twelve-week course of Positive Intelligence (PQ). The PQ training was developed and led by Shirzad Chamine, author, resident Stanford lecturer, and former CEO of the largest coach-training organization Co-Active Training Institute (CTI). PQ measures the percentage of time your mind is serving you as opposed to sabotaging you. While your IQ and EQ (emotional intelligence) contribute to your maximum potential, it is your PQ that determines how much of that potential you actually achieve.[3]

Chamine teaches us all about our nine saboteurs, their negative effects on self-love, and what to do to counteract them. These saboteurs can look like many different things, but regardless of the type of negative energy they bring, they keep us from moving forward. Some of the top personal saboteurs I see in myself and clients for instance are: people pleasing, victim, and avoider.

At the heart of it these saboteurs are the damaging voices of these self-critics in our heads that hold us back. They stab us with hurtful words like "You are not doing enough. You are not good enough. Why would you even try?" This is neither healthy nor helpful. The PQ process teaches us to instead lean into our PQ sage muscle. The Sage is that wise voice inside of us that helps handle challenges with a clear and calm mind along with positive emotions. The sage is firmly rooted in self-compassion, understanding, self-forgiveness, and overall positive vibes. Sage is way more fun. Choose sage!

Erin is a licensed psychologist with experience helping clients navigate self-negativity. She believes clients who intently listen to all parts of themselves—including the negative parts—with understanding and curiosity achieve the best outcomes. Rather than burying these feelings, clients who regularly check in with themselves develop a higher level of self-awareness, ultimately enabling them to unlock the elusive key to true happiness.

She explains that it is all about having a healthy relationship with yourself, and she does this through leveraging her expertise with Internal Family Systems (IFS). IFS is a transformative tool that conceives of every human being as a system of protective and wounded inner parts led by a core self. They believe the mind is naturally multiple, which is a good thing. "Just like members of a family, inner parts are forced from their valuable states into extreme roles within us. Self is in everyone, and it can't be damaged." It knows how to heal. We just need to listen to it.[4]

Here's how Erin describes the process: "Think about it like your average family. We are all individually layered just like families are. Each family has one kid who's the hero and everyone celebrates, one kid who's the joker, and one kid who's the problem child.

"If you look at a lot of families, you will see that within them people often take on multiple versions of these roles. Sometimes these roles shift, but the key is that within each of us exists a multitude of roles, each serving a different purpose. Some of our parts are bold, some parts are scary, and some parts protect other parts. Instead of being hard on the parts of us that are angry with us, we need to lovingly speak to them. We need to understand that it is their job to help and protect us. We should be thankful for them, listen to them, and allow them to protect us."

Not only does Erin practice IFS with her clients, but she also applies it to her own life. Recently, she shared a vulnerable story with me about her inner dialogue. One morning, while getting ready, she felt unsettled and couldn't pinpoint the unmet need that was causing her anxiety. She had a huge day ahead of her and paused, suddenly knowing exactly what she needed to do.

Instead of feeling anger and frustration with herself, she took a deep breath and began to lean in to curiously listen to herself. At that point, she started her own powerful inner dialogue. She lovingly asked herself, "What would I tell the inner stressed out me right now?"

Through a series of questions and answers, it finally came to her. "She needs to just put one foot in front of the other, and that means starting with getting dressed. So I would tell her to get dressed." Relief washed over her as she felt her anxiety dissipate. Although simple, sometimes finding the next best move can be almost impossible when you are feeling overwhelmed. As her shoulders relaxed and she headed toward her closet, she knew it would all be okay and the day would unfold exactly as it was meant to.

> **Ignite the Spark:** If you want to experiment with practicing self-compassion, begin by increasing your awareness of those negative thoughts and curiously listen to them. When you hear them start to creep in, you have the power to reframe them. Do this through reminding yourself that you are worthy, talented, and perfect just the way you are. Give it a try and capture your reflections!

## ABANDON (AND UNPLUG): FEAR

Fear of failure is another huge obstacle that often gets in our way. Fear can be like this heavy cloud hanging over our heads, making us second-guess every step we take toward our goals. It sneaks in whispering doubts in our ears and making us question our abilities, reminding us it is always easier to stick to what we know, even if it means settling for less than what we truly want. But here's the kicker: When we let fear call the shots, we end up stuck in this loop of "what ifs" and "could have beens." We miss out on chances to grow, to learn, and to chase after those big dreams we deserve and the world needs.

As Tesla and SpaceX founder Elon Musk famously said, "If things aren't failing, you're not innovating enough." Yet 43 percent of entrepreneurs "fear failure, despite evidence that business owners should be comfortable with failure and learn from the experience."[5]

This is a place where our internal competing commitments show up. We want to chase those big dreams, yet at the same time we are terrified of embarrassing ourselves. This leads to us living a life with one foot on the gas and one on the brake, leaving us immobile despite wanting our dreams so badly

Thomas Edison is often credited with saying, "I have not failed. I've just found ten thousand ways that won't work." I love this quote because it reframes the story. It is not about the light bulb in the end but all of the failure and perseverance.[6]

Edison's journey to invent the electric light bulb was marked by numerous setbacks and failures. He conducted thousands of experiments, each time encountering new challenges and setbacks. However, instead of being discouraged by his failures, Edison viewed them as essential steps toward success. He learned from each attempt, refining his approach and pushing forward despite setbacks.

Through unwavering determination and resilience, Edison finally succeeded in creating a practical and commercially viable light bulb. His triumph not only illuminated the world but also served as a timeless example of how perseverance and a positive attitude toward failure can lead to extraordinary achievements.

Edison's story continues to inspire people today, reminding us that failure is not the end but rather a crucial part of the journey toward success. It highlights the importance of resilience, persistence, and an unwavering belief in one's abilities to overcome obstacles and achieve greatness.

That sounds simple. Right? Well, just because it is simple does not mean it is not hard. Overcoming fear of failure takes rewiring the brain and reframing our thinking.

## REWIRE FEAR: LEARNER'S MINDSET

The first trick to overcoming the fear of failure is cultivating a learner's mindset.[7] When we adopt a learner's mindset, we are reframing our approach to every new experience as an opportunity to learn. Instead of responding to new experiences with judgment, which—let's be real—is what we have likely done in the past, we can more easily adapt to our surroundings and absorb information by leaning into our journey with curiosity.

So what could this look like? Instead of approaching a situation by saying, "I have tried it all, and nothing is working," you start by asking yourself, "What learning could come from this failure? What can I take with me to my next experience that builds on this and allows me to grow? What are a few small experiments that I can try to fail fast and learn from?"

Every time something goes a little sideways, instead of getting frustrated or feeling the weight of failure, my business partner and I say, "Look at us learning." It changes the whole game.

> **Ignite the Spark:** Something to try here is reflecting and capturing through a learner's mindset. This exercise involves reflection and writing prompts designed to help you embrace challenges, learn from setbacks, and foster a growth-oriented perspective.
>
> This can be a quick fifteen- to twenty-minute time set aside to reflect on a recent challenge or setback. Start by writing a brief description of the challenge. Be specific about what happened and how it made you feel.

Then take time to acknowledge any negative emotions such as frustration, disappointment, or self-doubt. Once you have given yourself a moment, begin moving into learner mode.

Use this time to consider and capture what you learned from the experience and the skills you gained as well as what did and didn't work. Try to consider alternative perspectives like: What else could you have tried? What else could be true? Consider what stories you may be telling yourself that are untrue and no longer serving you. Ask yourself how viewing the situation through a learner's mindset might help you approach future challenges with confidence and curiosity.

Most importantly, become aware of how these insights helped you to learn about yourself. Focus on the positive aspects of the experience and how it contributed to your growth and development. Based on your reflections, identify specific goals or actions you can take to further develop your skills and abilities. Recognize that setbacks are a natural part of the learning process, and your worth is not defined by your achievements or failures. Treat yourself with the same kindness and understanding you would offer to a friend facing similar challenges.

At the end of the day, can you imagine what a life could look like where you live from a vantage point of learning and growth, and fear is no longer part of your vocabulary? Letting go of fear is the gateway to achieving your dreams. It's about embracing vulnerability, stepping out of your comfort zone, overcoming obstacles, and getting out of your own way. When you move from fear to learning, you open yourself up to new possibilities and opportunities and release its grip on you. By cultivating courage, perseverance, and a positive mindset, you empower yourself to pursue your dreams, and that growth energy will now be the catalyst for transformation.

## ABANDON (AND UNPLUG): SOCIETAL EXPECTATIONS

In the book *Immunity to Change,* authors Robert Kegan and Lisa Laskow Lahey address societal pressures and their impact on us. These societal pressures affect our hidden assumptions that drive behavior because our assumptions are shaped not only by personal experiences but also by societal norms, values, and expectations. As such, societal pressure to conform to certain standards of success shape our beliefs about what is possible or permissible as individuals.

Social conditioning is another way external expectations can limit or guide us. Social norms can create resistance to change by reinforcing existing behaviors and attitudes. For instance, societal pressure to maintain a certain image or status quo can make it difficult for individuals to break entrenched patterns of behavior, making it almost impossible to live what is then considered an unconventional, although likely fulfilling, life. In short, we have a fear of being judged.

Collective mindsets within organizations and communities also influence our decision-making processes and behavior, making it difficult for individuals to challenge the status quo. Understanding and addressing these collective mindsets to facilitate meaningful change at both the individual and organizational levels is key.

Overall, *Immunity to Change* suggests that societal pressures play a significant role in shaping individual and organizational behavior. By identifying and understanding the influence of societal norms and expectations, individuals and organizations can begin to challenge existing assumptions and create environments that are more conducive to personal and collective growth.[8]

My hypothesis is that we all experience some degree of confusion about what we truly want and how to fight for it. In the absence of clarity, we follow this American Dream of what we think success should be—up and to the right, more things, more money, bigger titles, and keeping up with the Joneses.

Stephen Covey, a well-known author and educator, best recognized for his influential book *The 7 Habits of Highly Effective People*, studied the evolution of the definition of success. He researched more than two hundred years of self-improvement, self-help, and popular psychology literature to analyze and understand it. Covey noticed a stark historical contrast between two types of success.

Before World War I, success was attributed to ethics of character—such as humility, fidelity, integrity, courage, and justice. Yet after the war, we shifted to the personality ethic. This shift defined success as a function of personality, public image, behaviors, and skills. This shift led us to shallow, quick successes as well as overlooking the deeper principles of life.

Even when he published his book in 1989, Covey saw that this was leading to an epidemic of high achievers plagued with a sense of emptiness.[9]

Research on this continues, and very clear data points illustrate the exponential growth of this trend. With the definition of success we are all adopting, we are losing our way in what we truly should be pursuing.

In their book, *Designing Your Life: How to Build a Well-Lived, Joyful Life,* coauthors and educators on design thinking, Bill Burnett and Dave Evans, observed, "Our research suggests that 80 percent of all people of all ages don't really know what they are passionate about." In addition, "In the US, only 27 percent of college graduates end up in a career related to their major."[10]

## REWIRE SOCIETAL EXPECTATIONS: CALLING YOUR SUCCESS SHOT

I love this quote from the book by Timber Hawkeye, *The Opposite of Namaste*: "I wonder if we try to find ourselves through the years or if we actually already know who we are but since the world tells us to 'fit in' we basically audition for different roles until we nail one that gets us the standing ovation and that's the role we commit to playing."[11]

I think he is right. Not only are we told what fitting in and winning looks like, but we are also applauded for what we are good at, when in reality that may not be what we are passionate about at all. Success is about achieving goals that truly matter, but it's essential that these goals align with our own passions and values, not those imposed by others. True success comes from pursuing what we deeply care about, making the journey both meaningful and fulfilling.

But how do we do that, and what does that mean? Well, we accomplish this through creating, owning, and calling our own success shot. Calling your own success shot is creating a clear, concise sentence or two that outlines your unique and personal idea of success for your life. If you were able to live out your legacy and bring what you are most passionate about to the table, what would that be?

It doesn't have to be perfect. It just has to feel good. When we talk about success in our life, it should be more about how writing it makes you feel, how it lights you up, and how you are energized to chase it. Mine changes slightly every year. Yours may or may not, but I like the variation as I grow and change. Right now, for instance, my statement is: "I am healthy and strong, a leader in experience creation, and I inspire people to transform their lives."

Now, of course, I have many more goals for the year—like publishing this book, launching a podcast, and so on. But the true definition that stands on top of it all is nailing that success shot. It is at the core of what lights me up.

A few short years ago, my focus was on title and money, which isn't right or wrong; there's no judgment if those matter most to you. Now, my priority is serving others. While money remains important because it fuels my "experience creation," it no longer drives what I choose to do. Instead, this input enables me to do meaningful things with those I love.

The question I often get here is: "What if the thing I am passionate about doesn't deliver what I need from a compensation or external validation perspective?" To this I say a few things.

First, it's possible to pursue your passion part time or as a side hustle as you continue working at a job that offers you the financial stability you need. This allows you to enjoy the best of both worlds without sacrificing your livelihood, and eventually, over time, you will build your business and can phase out the work you no longer love.

Additionally, exploring fields related to your passion that may offer more stable compensation or recognition than your original idea can be a wise strategy. An example here may be that you have a passion for music but are unsure how to break out as a paid musician. You could explore roles teaching, writing music reviews, or producing music while you build your art and portfolio on the side. Doing this brings you closer to what matters most while also enabling you to enter relevant circles and make connections that could eventually pay off.

The other thing that often happens when we try something new is that those around you may judge or not understand why you are taking an unconventional path or, in other words, changing your energy yet still thriving in your given culture and environment.

This can be a tough one. Have you heard the crabs in the pot analogy? When a single crab tries to escape from a pot, the others pull it back down, ensuring nobody escapes. This metaphor is all about how the people around us are confused or threatened by this new version of us and may feel "less than" when we try to rise. Instead of supporting us, they try to put doubt in our way, make negative remarks, and hold us back.

In the end, it is our life to live, and outside of being a complete societal derelict, beating to your own drum and bringing your own Big Energy is absolutely what the world needs. You may outgrow your group as you change and excel, and you may surround yourself with new likeminded people.

While it may seem sad to move on, I think being stuck in the life you are supposed to have because you are too scared to be the real you and define your success in a way that differs from others is even sadder. The philosopher and entrepreneur Matshona Dhliwayo says it best: "You don't excel by conforming to society. You excel by conforming to your higher self."[12]

> **Ignite the Spark:** Now take a second to really think about what calling your own success shot looks like for you. How will you define your own success and happiness? You may want to try on multiple sentences before revisiting and playing around with which elements you want to edit, combine, and finalize. I recommend you pause here and complete the exercise before moving on.

### EXPECT TO BE DERAILED
When abandoning things, it can be really freakin' hard, and I get that, but carrying that same old baggage into a season

we are no longer in just does not serve us. So be prepared that you will likely resist change, and know it may take some time to rewire old well-worn patterns. When you trip, fall, and get derailed due to circumstances, I just ask that you do your best to get back up and try again.

Personally, I experienced this in the hardest way. After my cancer treatment in 2017 and feeling sorry for myself for a few minutes—well, almost two years, really—I was finally ready to rebuild. So I did all the work on the internal blockers through educating myself and diving into personal development and therapy work. I removed bad coping behaviors like too much drinking and wasting hours on social media.

In turn, I built in incredible daily habits and routines by getting up at 6:00 a.m. and following a very strict two-hour schedule rooted in physical and emotional health as well as intense personal development. As I talked about in the previous chapter, the results were incredible. I was literally living my best life. Then COVID-19 hit...

The world was terrifying, my job was impossible, and I was homeschooling three young kids. But more importantly, I was trying to balance all of their mental health from the anxiety, fear, and loss of their friends. We were in a period of grieving and trying to understand what even mattered anymore. What did a size four with big goals to run her own media company matter if half the population was going to die and we could never leave our house again?

So each day started to slip away, and we moved to the lake house, where I no longer had access to our home gym; we certainly couldn't go to a gym even if our tiny lake town had one. Some days, the girls and I did yoga and went for runs when the weather finally allowed.

But to be honest, at one point, I just gave up on growing myself and investing in my health. I turned it in for the much easier glass of wine or the mindless two hours of putting a puzzle together. When the days turned cold, months later without a change of view, we bought an RV and moved ourselves to the Florida Keys, where we lived every day like it may potentially be our last day. I lost sight of the fit, strong, inspired business-building woman I had created, and I turned her into a survivor, a mother, a camp counselor, a therapist, and whatever else we needed on the road.

I don't regret the evolution of my roles during this season; I was exactly where I needed to be. However, reflecting on where I was in 2019, I'm saddened by the decline and feel a strong need to rebuild. I refuse to let being derailed mean that I am giving up completely. It is easy to become discouraged when a derailing happens, but I live by the Chinese proverb, "The best time to plant a tree was twenty years ago. The second-best time is now."

So when we are trying to change, things will get in your way, and it is best to call those out so you can devise ways to work through them. At the end of the day, living a life that you are passionate about takes hard work, and the path will have obstacles. However, in the end, we have to ask ourselves: Isn't the price of it worth it tenfold?

If you get derailed, go back to the start of the SPARK process and begin again. It is never too late to transform.

**CHANGE IS HARD**

Leslie knows what she needs to do to change her lifestyle and become healthier. She knows it starts with the right foods, water, sleep, and exercise. But Leslie is a forty-seven-year-old mom of four, who works full time, cares for her ailing mother, and does not have a spare minute to take care of herself. Time and again, she tries to carve out fitness time and buys healthy groceries, but then she slips back into old habits of eating fast food on the go or the kids' leftovers.

She knows she needs to change but has no idea how to pivot her life in such a wide arc. The story she tells herself each week is that if she can just get through this week, she will make better choices and change her approach to find one that works. But weeks turn into years, and before Leslie even notices, she has gained ten more pounds, and her lab results continue to decline at her annual visit. Her energy is completely drained, and she feels overwhelmed and stuck. Sound familiar at all?

It's not Leslie's fault, and if you're experiencing the same struggle, it's not your fault either. Change is super hard for so many reasons, including the rat race of life as we try to "have it all." Change is scientifically hard, given how we are wired as human beings.

As a mom with two high schoolers in AP psychology, I am learning all about avoidance conditioning. Avoidance conditioning is the establishment of a behavior that prevents or postpones aversive stimulation. This involves the learning of a behavior to prevent an aversive stimulus or consequence or avoid it through escaping the unpleasant situation.[13]

Because change is hard, we do all we can to avoid it and instead burrow back under the covers of our comfort zones.

It is hard to see my client Candace struggle with this. Candace hates confrontations and especially dreads experiencing any version of them at work. So whenever a challenging situation arises, like giving feedback to her teammates, Candace literally feels sick with discomfort and anxiety.

One day, during a team meeting, Candace notices that when she stays silent and avoids contributing to the discussion, the tension dissipates, and she manages to avoid conflict. Gradually, this pattern becomes so ingrained in her behavior that she even finds excuses to skip meetings to evade uncomfortable situations.

When she comes to me to work on this, Candace knows her avoidance is hindering her professional growth and is well aware of the importance of active participation, but she's unsure how to break this unproductive pattern. Only by abandoning old stories and pushing herself to practice confrontation outside of her comfort zone can she begin to make real and lasting progress.

So you see, we are conditioned from the time we are young children to protect ourselves from danger and escape what is unknown versus embracing the openness of change.

Although we consciously desire our new and improved life and are committed to making a change, our deeply ingrained, unconscious assumptions act as a kind of immune system, attempting to shield us from the discomfort or perceived threats associated with change.

In one study conducted by the National Institute of Health, coronary bypass patients were told if they did not change their habits and embrace a new lifestyle, they would be in grave danger. Two years later, 90 percent of patients hadn't made the changes warranted. Said differently, 90 percent of the participants in the study would rather die than change. This phenomenon underscores the formidable challenge of behavior change, even in the face of life-threatening circumstances. It speaks to the complexities of human psychology, including factors such as denial, resistance to change, and the allure of familiar patterns, which can outweigh the rational understanding of the need for change.[14]

This is one of the biggest reasons people seek out the help of a coach. They need a catalyst to help them get unstuck and head toward the goals they have been unable to achieve. We help them to continue trying, testing, and experimenting until eventually they can navigate through the murky waters of change and transform forever.

The last story I want to share on the topic of abandoning and unplugging is that of Winston. In our very first coaching session, we were exploring his fear of rejection and how that was holding him back. Forty minutes into our session, he was on the brink of happy tears: "I feel liberated, like the weight of twenty men has been lifted off my shoulders. My deep belief that I had to carry everyone and have all the answers fueled my fear of rejection. Now, I realize it's not about always having the answers or carrying others. I'm free to offer ideas and lead from behind. I can finally chase my dreams without restraint."

In that moment, he realized that letting go of what held him back opened the door to infinite other opportunities. I want you to experience that same liberation, embracing the freedom to achieve the future and dreams you truly deserve.

I believe in you! A whole new, vibrant life awaits once you abandon and unplug your energy drainers. Anything at all is possible for you as you continue to consistently rewire and get back up when things are tough.

Now let's take action and get those results...

**CHAPTER 6**

# RESULTS

―

*"Today is when everything that's going to happen from now on begins."*

—HARVEY FIRESTONE JR.

In the "Purpose" chapter, we discussed setting your goals. In this chapter, we are going to work together to crush them! Getting the results you want takes work. In other words, we are going to explore what you may still need to learn, do, develop, or put into place to move your dreams to goals and your goals to action and success.

Driving results requires a clear vision and a strategic approach. It's not just about setting goals but about understanding the actionable steps needed to achieve them. In this section, we'll explore the methods and strategies that will guide us, ensuring we stay focused, adaptable, and aligned with our purpose. Together, we'll chart a course that turns ambition into measurable success.

## HEALTH AND WELL-BEING

Body. Mind. Soul. Overall well-being is at the epicenter of all we do. Without creating and cultivating our energy, we have nothing to run on. Just like cars can't run without gas, our dreams can't come true if we don't have a strong foundation to build from.

As an added value, have you ever heard someone say their big bright idea came to them while they were running? Or in the shower? Or during meditation? This phenomenon of ideas emerging during activities is due to the mind's state of relaxation and reduced cognitive load during these moments of solitude or physical exertion.

Engaging in these activities allows your subconscious mind to wander freely, unburdened by distractions and pressures. Think of it like a mental liberation that gives you fertile ground for creativity and insight, enabling connections between disparate thoughts and concepts to form more fluidly.

As your mind wanders during exercise or meditation, it sifts through memories, experiences, and observations, often coming up with novel perspectives and solutions to problems you have been laboring over. These moments of clarity highlight the importance of allowing ourselves the space for reflection and to take care of our body and mind, as these moments fuel our energy creation that is needed to spark the best versions of our minds!

Some of the best ways to focus on your well-being are moving your body, embracing a healthy diet, drinking half your body weight in ounces of water, and getting your fair share of sleep.

Yes, I know you all know this. But we need to do these things, even if we do not want to or aren't feeling it, because without strong well-being, literally nothing is possible for a sustained amount of time.

By committing to these life-giving initiatives, you are constantly replenishing your energy source and creating a flywheel for passion and dreams to be built on.

Moving your body for at least thirty minutes a day is also the best thing you can do to improve your mood and increase your energy. A study done by the *Harvard Business Review* found that participants who engaged in more physical exercise had an increased level of performance at work and increased motivation.[1]

Exercise has also been said to help with enhanced imagination, increased creativity, and innovation by boosting blood flow and oxygen levels in the brain, removing toxins from the body.

Eating right is about giving your body the fuel it needs to run at an optimal level and provide what you need in terms of energy. Eating well is intricately linked to achieving professional goals as it directly influences cognitive function and energy levels. A nutritious diet gives you the nutrients and fuel to create and sustain your mental energy and clarity. The American Society for Nutrition shared that "increased fruit and vegetable consumption positively impacts psychological health, and daily vegetable consumption has a therapeutic impact by reducing symptoms of depression in people with clinical depression."[2]

So if food can have that deep of an impact on our mental health, imagine what it can do for our professional brain power in terms of concentration and productivity throughout the day. Good food even enhances our ability to focus on tasks, make informed decisions, and adapt to challenges effectively.

Drinking half your body weight in ounces of water will change your life. It matters because it helps maintain proper hydration levels, supports bodily functions, promotes overall health, and helps you just feel better all the time. Use water to replace your soda, your second cup of coffee, and even alcohol—not always easy but 100 percent worth it.[3]

Take my client Eileen, for example. Eileen is a successful C-level executive. She is that woman who is always put together, has the perfect look, and is wicked smart at board meetings—a real, get-it-all-done kind of lady. Yet she was severely struggling with focus, which was affecting her ability to up-level and be more strategic.

Not surprisingly, she was overall just burned out. We worked through many different ways to increase her performance, but when she started to explore what her level of exercise and overall health focus looked like, she laughed at me and asked, "Are you my coach or my doctor?"

Clearly not a doctor, but having seen how important health and energy creation is, I explained all of the benefits and studies above with her. Finally, she reluctantly agreed to try a few experiments over the following month. The only rule was that each day, in addition to moving her body for thirty minutes, she would explore one additional health-based habit.

I asked her to keep a journal on what she noticed about her energy and cognitive abilities. When she worked out prior to a big presentation, did she see a difference? When she got a strong night's sleep—skipping late-night Netflix and spiking her energy with three morning coffees—did her brain fire stronger and faster as she designed her annual business plan? She tried various new activities, really paying attention to what she saw and capturing things she learned.

At first, it was challenging for her to find time for it amid her busy schedule, but she quickly started to see the rewards of her labor. Even a short week after making these well-being habits a priority, she noticed a difference in her attitude, clarity in the work she produced, and surprisingly to her—increased creativity. She found that her daily runs helped her clear her mind, reduce stress, and boost her energy levels. She even began to look forward to this time and found that the time spent exercising allowed her to focus more effectively during the day and approach challenges with a renewed sense of clarity and purpose.

> **Ignite the Spark:** I encourage you to lovingly challenge yourself to adopt new well-being habits. Make space to experiment with different options, reflect on what resonates with you, and start experiencing the rewards of treating your mind, body, and soul in a way that allows them to best support you in return.

### LEARNING AND DEVELOPMENT
Skills and additional schooling or training can help tremendously in moving toward goals. As a coach, I am deeply

invested in helping clients acquire new skills, knowledge, and competencies needed to achieve their personal or professional growth objectives. This piece is personal because going back to get an MBA may make sense for one person based on their finances and family life while gaining more hands-on experience may make more sense for another.

Even engaging in self-directed learning activities to enhance your abilities and expertise can work effectively. Continued learning not only helps to unlock our goals but pushes us outside of our comfort zone, connecting us with a new community. In short, it can be a pretty fun way to get our brains firing in new directions.

A large portion of my business is leading group coaching programs at major universities for their graduate programs. My sweet spot is with executive MBA and professional MBA programs, where students already have significant work experience but seek additional "power" skills and knowledge for various reasons. These reasons include making more money at their job, getting a new job, moving up, or simply continuing to grow and learn. The common thread is that all of these students are, for the first time in years, experiencing a blend of excitement and apprehension as they embark on learning a wide range of new concepts.

Adult learning, however, is very different, and we found that the group coaching element is a game-changer. It is all about experimenting with things, working together to overcome challenges, and ultimately, leveraging the powerful wisdom of the collective group. Adult learning differs from the traditional education of our youth because it focuses on real-world application and self-directed exploration. Its value lies in fostering practical skills, enhancing professional growth, and empowering individuals to adapt and thrive in diverse personal and professional contexts throughout their lives. Continuously learning new skills and seeking training, even after years of work experience, is paramount in today's rapidly evolving professional landscape.

Ryan initially struggled to embrace adult learning, especially when it came to critical interpersonal skills—or "power" skills, as we like to call them. These skills can be challenging because vulnerability is essential for success and crucial for growth. During a training session with him and his fellow leaders, it was clear from the start that he was holding back, appearing distracted, and not fully present with the group. Since group coaching thrives on the inclusion of all voices to bring diverse experiences and thoughts to the table, my partner and I consistently encouraged his participation. Eventually, he began to open up, sharing more and actively engaging with his peers.

During our check-out question "What will you take away from today?" he even started to share in meaningful ways. In the end, what we thought was resistance was just his perception of what our time together would look like. In his mind, he anticipated that we would do all the talking and, as instructors, would have all the answers versus us facilitating a collective engaged conversation where all participants learn from each other.

This becomes especially important when you are transitioning, like during this SPARK Energy Transformation Process. It means not being afraid of breaking into a new industry, role, or job that is unknown but instead getting curious about the skill and training you need to up-skill yourself to be effective and then leaning into that. It also means being open to learning, knowing you bring rich experiences to the table and you will be able to add and take value to grow.

As seasoned professionals, we understand the value of our existing expertise, yet embracing new knowledge opens doors to fresh perspectives, innovation, and adaptability. In a world where industries transform, technologies evolve, and methodologies shift, our commitment to learning becomes the cornerstone of staying relevant and competitive.

By investing in ongoing education and skill development, we not only enhance our professional capabilities but also invigorate our passion for growth and discovery. Embracing lifelong learning fosters resilience, empowers us to navigate change with confidence, and positions us as agile contributors in an ever-changing workforce.

As seasoned practitioners, we recognize that the journey of learning is perpetual, and our willingness to embrace new skills ensures we remain agile, inspired, and primed for success in the dynamic landscape of tomorrow.

I never imagined I would be building websites for the first time at almost fifty, but as a new entrepreneur, here I am—learning and experimenting.

## HABITS

Heather knows all about habits. Most notably, how to create strong habits that focus on her health in a consistent fashion. Twelve years ago, Heather began a weight loss journey that led to her losing two hundred pounds. Even though that in and of itself is an incredible success, her continued dedication led to her keeping it off for ten years. As a single mom of five—yes, you heard right, five daughters—she says the secret sauce is to show up every single day, both for herself and to be a role model for her daughters.

I originally started following Heather on social media where I read her inspirational story. I was able to watch her from the sidelines, year after year, as she stuck with her goals and expanded her scope by influencing others and becoming a role model to women looking to do the same. She has crafted a big, beautiful, healthy life based on her dedication to her small habits every single day. Without these habits, she would have slipped back into old patterns and never have achieved the sustainability she now effortlessly embraces.

A lot of science is actually rooted in neurological pathways and habit formation, with studies being published through many scholarly articles, including the National Library of Medicine. These studies show that the brain is highly adaptable, forming neural pathways based on repeated behaviors, which leads to the creation of habits. Once these habits are established, they create strong neural connections.[4]

Breaking these connections requires incredibly conscious effort and time to establish new, healthier pathways. Often, these habits begin innocently enough, but they gradually consume the time and energy that could be better spent pursuing our big dreams and moving toward the life we desire.

Over time it becomes easier to lean into our bad habits that become well-worn paths, using them to numb, mask, and in the end avoid the harder things needed to tackle and enable our growth and development. These habits may look like eating, binging, streaming, drinking, and working too much.

Habits are also reinforced by the brain's reward system, releasing feel-good neurotransmitters like dopamine that make it very hard to compete with. What is easier, a glass of wine or heading out to the gym for an hour? We want the quick hit. But transforming our lives is not a quick hit. Nonetheless, I promise you will get dopamine hits along the way. It just may take some patience and time.

Building these habits is a gradual and intentional process that starts with understanding the cues, routines, and rewards behind behaviors. When working with my clients, I begin by helping them define their goal. Then we identify specific habits they can experiment with to achieve that goal through manageable steps. Regularly tracking these steps is the most reliable path to success.

First, find an annual vision goal. Then split it out quarterly, monthly, and daily. This keeps your goal in focus every single day, and eventually you accomplish your small steps so many times that they no longer seem like anything other than a natural habit—like brushing your teeth. Consistency is key, so aim for small, regular actions that align with their larger goals and ultimately the why.

Positive reinforcement is crucial in establishing habits, so acknowledge your progress and celebrate small victories. Acknowledging and celebrating your achievements, even the small ones along the way, is key for continued momentum and motivation. Positive reinforcement strengthens your habit loop and helps you continue making progress, and darn it is so fun!

With my twenty-four for 2024 goal I mentioned, I have a daily checklist of my eight habits in my planner. When I get to the end of the week and have them checked off, I reward myself with things like a new rug for my office, organizing containers for my jewelry, and so on. I choose easy stuff in the beginning and then eventually move into bigger rewards, like new clothes for my book tour when I hit bigger milestones. I even created a master rewards wish list on Amazon that I can choose from each week and month. I am a fan of smaller rewards with smaller windows so that we 1) don't break the bank but also 2) aren't waiting too long for that "joy bomb" for the hard work put in. Early and often for small wins is key!

Additionally, create a supportive environment that minimizes obstacles and encourages the desired behavior. This may be as simple as cleaning off your writing desk the night before or making sure your fitness tracker is charged to capture your training runs. Pro tip: I always set up my coffee machine the night before so I just hit grind when I wake up, and the smell inspires me. This routine makes me feel productive right away and frees up time to get into my first job of the day—waking up my eleven-year-old with a motivational daily celebration.

In the book *Atomic Habits,* James Clear provides a transformative guide for seeking positive change in people's lives through habits. He emphasizes the power of small changes and habits due to their profound impact on our lives.

Clear also shares with us the OAES method, which simply means we need to make our habits obvious, attractive, easy, and satisfying. By implementing his framework, we are able to create environments and routines that support positive behavior change, ultimately leading to sustainable habits and long-term success.

Clear says, "Every action you take is a vote for the type of person you wish to become. No single instance will transform your beliefs, but as the votes build up, so does the evidence of your new identity."[5] I admire his way of thinking because he essentially shows us that our habits shape our identity, and by consistently aligning our actions with the person we aspire to be, we gradually reinforce a new identity and belief system.

Another great tool he leverages is cue, routine, and reward loop: identifying the trigger (cue) for a habit, establishing a routine, and associating it with a positive outcome (reward) helps in reinforcing the habit loop; and lastly, linking it back to your bigger why, as I like to say, or as Clear shares, undergoing an identity change.

True behavior change comes from a shift in identity when we concentrate intensely on becoming the type of person we want to be and living the life we want. By aligning habits with our "why" and our identity with these habits, we are more likely to maintain momentum and build on these positive changes over the long term.[6]

As a visual person, I personally like to create a diagram of building blocks, each one a small habit that stacks upon another and builds up to what I want to achieve. For example, in writing this book, I knew I had to find the time to make it happen. Even though I was motivated and excited about the work, with my busy life of being a mom and building a business, I was aware that time and energy may be limited.

So I put together a diagram of what my habit stacking would look like to accomplish it. First, I pre-calendared my workouts (to increase energy). Then I added on my dedicated (also calendared) writing time in places that invigorated me (various fun coffee shops). Then the final block was to get into the habit of writing every day (even if it sucked, even if the words were not flowing). Learning and stacking these habits will move me from the 81 percent of people who have writing a book on their bucket list to the 2 percent who actually publish one. Incremental habits lead to big dreams coming true.

> **Ignite the Spark:** Begin revisiting the vision, purpose, why, and goals you established earlier in the SPARK process, and pencil in the habit that will help you get there. In addition to tracking them, I love a good if-then exercise. If you want to accomplish something, what else needs to be true? For example, if I want to work out at 6:00 a.m., then I need to be in bed by 11:00 p.m. If I need

> to be in bed by 11:00 p.m., then I need to be off screens by 10:00 p.m., and so on. This is a great way to help you understand what needs to be possible for your goals to happen, and it helps you to proactively understand what may get in your way so you have a good offense set up ahead of it.

A great saying by Peter Drucker is: "If you want something new, you have to stop doing something old."[7]

As habits become ingrained, they naturally contribute to your personal growth and well-being. Patience and persistence are key in building lasting habits that positively impact your life. As you diligently work toward your goals, a natural progression unfolds, guiding you to live more authentically. This journey of aligning values, setting goals, and forming habits deepens self-awareness and connects you to your why, intertwining your habits with the core of your authenticity. Ultimately, pursuing your goals and building habits becomes a holistic evolution of self-discovery and purposeful living.

The best version of me worked my way to a bikini body at forty-five with a body that had not seen a bikini since my honeymoon a good sixteen years earlier. It was over a full year of hard work and sticking to my goal of achieving it with the bikini hanging in my closet in front of me every morning along the way. Every single time I got the question "How did you do it?" I replied, "Habits." Consistency, day after day, is the foundation for building your most beautiful life.

**ENERGY HYPE SQUAD**

Investing in and expanding your network in an authentic way is one of most meaningful gifts you can give yourself as you move toward living the life you crave and deserve. Having a strong network and support system can significantly help you achieve your goals by providing you with access to resources, encouragement, constructive feedback, and advice on learning opportunities, and it can help you increase resilience and keep your momentum! Whether with job leads, mentorship, or advice, your network can open doors and help you progress toward your goals more efficiently.

Remember those SMART goals we talked about back in the "Purpose" chapter—and the increased likelihood of success when writing them down? Well, according to a study done by the American Society of Training and Development, you have a 65 percent chance of completing them when you publicly commit to your goals. And even better, if you have a specific accountability partner, that raises your chance of success to a whopping 95 percent.[8]

Building meaningful relationships and leveraging social capital are powerful motivators that can unlock significant opportunities on your journey. Through decades of experience, I've gained valuable insights in this area and even now offer group coaching sessions completely focused on building and maintaining your network.

I would actually credit the majority of my success in building my business, The BND Group, to navigating my network through revisiting relationships that I nurtured along the way or even reaching out to people from the past who I thought

I could learn from. Human interaction is still a thing we all crave. Even in a more virtual world, catching up with someone outside of your potentially mundane work day gives you a spark of inspiration and can refresh your perspective for the day, resetting you to think differently.

Good people want to help. They are honored to mentor you. It feels good to help people. We all know this. So asking will give people the chance to do something good and make a difference. If you have built a strong personal brand, you should leverage it, and people will be honored to sponsor you for opportunities.

Another thing I have learned along the way is that you likely have a big beautiful extended network too—the friends of your friends and contacts of your contacts. When you get that one-on-one time with your contacts, a final question you should always ask those people is, "Who else should I talk to?" and "Who else do you think could offer me some great advice (in the skill I am looking to build or the role I hope to explore)?" Be as specific as you can for what you are looking for, and don't be afraid to ask for a warm introduction.

When my daughters hesitate to ask for what they want, I ask them: "Who gets the biggest piece of cake?" The answer: "The one who asks for it." So you have to be brave. It can be scary to ask for it sometimes, but you don't need to do that immediately.

Take time to build and nurture your relationships over time, and be sure to create a shared value exchange before you make an ask. If someone does a favor for you, pay it forward.

If someone is taking the time to let you pick their brain, always ask how you can help them. There is always some way that you can help elevate their work or life, and asking shows you care and are invested in a long and prosperous partnership together.

Think of your network and community as your Energy Hype Squad (EHS). As you build your EHS, think about: 1) who should be in that closest circle; 2) what communities can you be a part of that inspire you to be a better person and help to increase your extended network circle; and 3) once you get into those rooms, what will you say?

In my opinion, you should have people on your EHS who fill these types of roles:

- The inspirer to continuously encourage you;
- The critic or challenger to give you hard feedback;
- The mentor to teach you;
- The sponsor or advocate to positively tell your story when you are not in the room;
- The accountability partner to keep you on track;
- A trusted person to have a different opinion or perspective from you; and
- Lastly, of course, a person to coach.

**Ignite the Spark:** Take a few minutes to sketch out what your EHS would look like if made up of these roles.

Lastly, setbacks and challenges are also inevitable on the journey toward achieving your goals, so having a strong support system can provide you with emotional support, guidance, and perspective during difficult times. This tribe you build will be critical in helping you navigate obstacles and bounce back stronger.

Once you start to expand your EHS to move out of your comfort zone and go to networking events like local events, clubs, and conferences, you need to have a solid intro.

What do you want people to know about you? What are your goals, and what is most important to you? Why should they help you? Take some time to think through the prompts of what this could look like. Think of it like a pitch. How do you get your EHS pumped to help you? And don't forget—how can you help them?

> **Ignite the Spark:** Try to sketch out your thirty-second introduction, either professionally or personally, and test it out on someone you trust. It should be clear, passionate, and reflect your why, not your what. We will do a deeper version of this in the "Kinetic Energy" chapter when we start to bring it all together to tell our story.

This can be an intimidating process, but you don't have to do it alone. A great benefit of enlisting a coach to help you on your journey is that our entire job is to unlock your development goals and dreams, so we are dedicated to making them happen. One of my favorite parts is helping my clients unlock their network and secure an advocate or sponsor to help elevate their exposure and growth. While the clients are still in the driver's seat of the actual outreach, through our work together, I help them identify mentor and sponsor opportunities as well as craft the ask in the most authentic way.

I have helped clients do this in several instances. A great example of this is the work with my client Connie. Connie is a doctor who is bright, energetic, self-assured, and incredibly impressive in her passions and goals. Yet when we talked about mentors and sponsors, she was at a loss. Who and how could she ask, and why would someone want to help her? Through our work together, we uncovered some very valuable patient advocacy work and research that Connie was engaging in. It provided an authentic way for her to open up a conversation with a rich value exchange between her and the hospital CEO, a female leader held in high esteem and whom Connie highly regarded. Through several meetings, the relationship continued to flourish, and before long Connie had not only secured an amazing mentor but a lifelong sponsor and advocate.

Without creating my own EHS, the book in your hands would never have been possible, and for that I am forever grateful and acutely aware of the importance of having a strong network.

**EXPERIMENTS**
Experiments foster growth by challenging us to step outside our comfort zones, explore new perspectives, and discover our untapped potential. They allow us to explore uncharted territories, challenge existing assumptions, and discover innovative approaches to accelerate our personal development.

I am always encouraging my clients to engage in safe-to-fail experiments, giving them the opportunity to play and grow without fear of failure. The term "safe-to-fail experiments" comes from the the Cynefin framework, which is a conceptual decision-making process created by Dave Snowden while he was at IBM Global Services.[9]

By conducting small-scale experiments to tackle an issue from different angles in a low-stakes environment, you can test ideas and remain open to new possibilities that may arise. In making these incremental changes, you can also learn, understand more about yourself, and push against your learning edge.

One of my favorite self-help books is Gretchen Rubin's *The Happiness Project*. In the book, Rubin shares her yearlong experiment to increase her happiness and provides advice for her readers on how to do the same. Rubin encourages readers to assess their own priorities, values, and goals and to take small, manageable steps toward positive change in their lives.

But what I love most about the book is the overarching theme of trying small, safe-to-fail experiments along the way. Each month, she chose to test out something new to boost her overall quality of life and happiness. She did this through cultivating various relationships, trying new hobbies, and focusing on joy in the everyday moments.

Through these experiments, she uncovered that small changes can lead to big results, and variations in daily habits, attitudes, and perspectives can have a significant impact on overall happiness and well-being. The key is to embrace the power of incremental progress and reap the benefit through the cumulative effect of positive changes over time.[10]

Monica knows all about experimenting, so I knew I had to interview her on this hot topic. Years ago, she made the courageous move to leave her job as an attorney and buy a fitness studio franchise—Burn Boot Camp. When I asked her to share her experimentation lessons learned along the way, she laughed and replied, "Well, the thing that jumps out to me is that the whole jump itself was one big experiment."

Monica believes in diving right in and giving things a try, because it's not about finding your passion; it's about letting your passion find you. And I believe embracing the courage to experiment and make bold moves is often the key to uncovering your true passion and purpose.

As a consumer of Burn Boot Camp for years, she fell in love with the community and eventually was approached to become an owner. She needed roughly thirty-odd skills to be successful, but she only possessed one—passion. She had faith in herself that she could learn the rest.

When taking on a massive life experiment like this, which meant draining her 401(k), the key for her was to shut out self-doubt and fear, believe in her own capabilities, and surround herself with like-minded "doers." In the end, her life mantra mirrors that of everyone at Burn transforming their lives: "She believed she could, so she did."

So in the end, when experimenting, you don't need to know all the things. I just ask that you try, learn, iterate, and explore from a place of abundance and curiosity. The goal here is just to learn more about yourself and start to understand what resonates. Be patient. This stuff does not happen overnight. After all, it is called work for a reason. The key is just to keep trying, because as Ralph Waldo Emerson said, "All life is an experiment. The more experiments you make the better."[11]

## GRATITUDE

Last winter, I was laid up. I mean back injured, leg injured, joints aching, heating pad kind of laid up. I still am not even sure how I got there. Let's just say I am no spring chicken anymore, and I just know I was in pain. My body was screaming at me, and my forty-nine years felt every bit north of seventy. Despite being known for my intense level of high inspirational energy, I couldn't leave my couch and was left feeling sorry for myself.

During this laid-up season, because I don't have an off-switch, I was scooting down the stairs on my tush to do laundry and clean the house and was organizing my daughter's closet from my seat on the floor. Looking back, I am sure my therapist would have a heyday with my inability to rest and allow my body to restore itself. But I felt I needed to be on the move at all times, doing everything at once.

So while laid up, I read, wrote, and took video calls in my PJs. I did, however, try to go to bed early, nourish my body, and drink tons of water. Finally, I woke up about five days later, and the pain was nearly nonexistent.

Everything was brighter. My coffee tasted better, my kids' voices sounded sweeter, and even the dog felt like more of a blessing, despite the endless task of letting him in and out—something that had felt overwhelming while I was injured.

I share this because it is so interesting how life works when you reach that Intensity Point and begin to realize you are expending your energy in all the wrong places. You realize that things you thought mattered, like a rude comment or a messy house, are irrelevant.

Y'all, none of that minutia matters. The world is so much bigger, and our life is so much richer! In the absence of real challenges, and I mean like real ones, our brains search for something to focus on. If we don't nourish our life with gratitude—in our relationships, our good health, and overall being connected to things we love—our brain will instead look to places of conflict and drama to keep busy.

The turning point for me was moving from frustration to deep, intentional gratitude. When we consciously make this shift and consistently anchor ourselves in thankfulness, it becomes nearly impossible to dwell on the negative.

Later that day, I needed gas for my car. So I entered the real world for the first time in almost a week. It was a total blessing—in fact, such a blessing I almost cried seeing all the people bustling and smiling at each other as the sun started to warm our frosting cars.

I was so deeply grateful to be upright and "normal," and I was grinning like crazy while taking it all in. I wanted to wave to people; heck, I really was feeling called to hug people or buy coffees for the next ten patrons.

It was like the environment and its players around me were showing up more clearly than I had seen in months, like a vivid technicolor dream. The energy was contagious. Slowly, I also realized the common shared thread. Everyone around me was serving the community in some way—post office drivers, police officers, construction, landscapers—and they were living in such joy. I felt a buzzing energy, like coworkers laughing and chatting as though they were at a fancy dinner party living in their heyday.

At that moment, I knew I had been too inwardly focused on challenges recently instead of basking in the fact that I am blessed to be living in my heyday, right now, today.

And it hit me. What if none of us realize we are living in our heyday until it's already past? What if we are missing the joy, thinking it will come at some later date when we have reached another self-imposed milestone along the way?

In college, I worked two jobs and took eighteen credit hours a semester to graduate from my university. It was intense as hell, but when I look back, it was my heyday. As a new mom learning the diapering, hearing the screaming, being puked on for a year and a half, that was my heyday. Before I heard the life-altering news that I had cancer and lived in an innocent bubble that health is endless until you are old, that was a total heyday. So I think you get it, and I certainly got the huge fat sign from the universe at that moment.

What if today is more of a heyday than tomorrow? And it likely is because, let's be real, we are all dying one day at a time, but in this relentless cycle of life, we often forget we are also living one day at a time.

So, I am left feeling that if we are not aware, open, and rooted in gratefulness, we miss it. If we are constantly in search of our future goal and that next big place or thing, we are missing the heyday we are living in.

I am not saying you shouldn't want more and strive for more. Look, I literally make a living helping people achieve audacious goals. But I am also saying indulge in the gift that is today.

Capitalize on today's energy and health, and be grateful for the prosperity you have both worked hard for and been gifted by the universe. Because it can change in an instant. Accidents happen, bad phone calls come in, health declines, people we love suffer or die, we have less money, we lose great jobs, we enter a global quarantine. You name it… things happen. There is never a "going back." There is never a return to "before," and we are only able to live in the after. So the only way to deal with that reality is to continue to appreciate the day that is today and remind ourselves that we are living in the heyday of our lives.

So the message here is while, yes, we are focusing on those hard-earned results, if we continue to embrace gratitude along the way, the journey will be sweeter and the results will feel even more rewarding.

## GRATITUDE PRACTICES

How can you create rituals to recognize your daily heyday and root in the gratefulness for your abundance and prosperity?

Practicing gratitude is critical to live your best life because it helps you build a positive mindset, increase your resilience, improve mental and physical health, and even increase your motivation to chase your goals.

In fact, research shows that practicing gratitude—fifteen minutes a day, five days a week—for at least six weeks can enhance mental wellness and promote a lasting change in perspective. Gratitude and its mental health benefits can also positively affect your physical health.[12]

A review of seventy various studies with more than twenty-six thousand people also found that higher levels of gratitude were associated with lower levels of depression.[13]

> **Ignite the Spark:** One way to root yourself in gratitude is through journaling. This type of journaling can be incredibly quick, so it can be done at the start of every day, during your morning routine, by writing down five things you are grateful for.
>
> But the twist is to try and choose things that have happened in the past day or so and are simple things, or as I call them "joy bombs." It could be a smile from a stranger that reminded you that kindness is alive. It could be the fifteen minutes you were able to build Legos with your daughter. We don't need big events and fancy

> things to be happy. Happiness is often more vibrant than ever in those everyday things and moments that bring us joy.

Other ways to practice gratitude include setting up a gratitude jar or starting a weekly gratitude text circle with close friends.

Gratitude jars work similarly to a piggy bank or coin box. Start by writing down things you're thankful for and placing them individually inside of your container. When you're feeling down or in need of motivation, you can pull one out to revisit. It can be a powerful reminder of how blessed you are. This is a great one to do as a family too.

A weekly gratitude text circle with close friends is a place where everyone can share messages of appreciation and acknowledge how fortunate you are to have each other. Appreciation texts or emails feel so good to both the receiver and the sender, and one small "I appreciate you and our friendship" note can make someone's entire day and yours too. Appreciation connections like this remind us that we are part of something bigger, we are not alone, and we have a community to love and support us. And what leads us to a better life than sharing in that?

I'll close this section on gratitude with a story: Each morning when I send my kids off, I say, "Something wonderful is going to happen today. Don't wait for it. Watch for it." By putting this thought into their minds, I help them focus on the joy around them rather than the negativity that often distracts us. The "watch for it" encourages them to stay open to positivity, knowing that actively seeking it brings great joy while passively waiting might cause them to miss it altogether.

Being grateful is a choice. Developing diligence and "watching for your wonderful" is just like any other muscle. You need to train it. But just like consistency in weight training, I promise you, it will be worth the reps you put in for the happiness outcome that you receive. Since we started this practice years ago, my kids still come home most days ready to share what they found. It matters.

Overall, all of this work can be challenging but also incredibly rewarding, leading to profound personal transformation and a deeper sense of connection. Yes, it takes courage, patience, and commitment, but the rewards are invaluable in terms of living a more authentic, meaningful, and fulfilling life.

As a reminder, these suggestions are meant to help you with the foundational elements of heeding the best results in your journey, yet they don't need to be done in any specific order or even all completed. They are simply here to help you think differently.

They are all opportunities to help you consider shaking up your life and pushing yourself out of that safe zone you may have been operating in for months, years, or perhaps decades. By allowing yourself to try some of these new and potentially uncomfortable experiences, you may feel fear, doubt, and all kinds of other things. But in the end, you will also experience surges of hope, pride in yourself, increased confidence and resilience, and just happiness.

You can do this—new things, hard things, anything. I just ask that you try, reflect, and check in. Then and only then can you decide what you keep and what you leave behind. Either way, you are headed forward in a newer, braver version of yourself on a path that is clearer with an energy currency that is wired for sustainable success.

Doesn't that sound incredible? Are you ready to turn the key and unlock the door to your most authentic life—one where you align with your purpose, craft your personal story, and bring it all together through harnessing your kinetic energy?

## CHAPTER 7

# KINETIC ENERGY

—

*"Don't be confused between what people say you are and who you know you are."*

—OPRAH

This chapter is about bringing the first four steps together, igniting momentum, and harnessing your kinetic energy. Kinetic energy is the force that emerges when you reflect deeply and step into your most authentic self. It's the driving power of living a life aligned with who you truly are.

As we explore in this chapter, authenticity, vulnerability, self-expression, value alignment, confidence, and owning your story are the essential elements in this process. Harnessing your kinetic energy means embracing the dynamic, ever-evolving nature of this journey—one that requires continual learning, adapting, and forward movement.

**AUTHENTICITY**

Imagine a world where you don't need anyone's permission to be exactly who you are, where other people's opinions of you neither matter nor distract you. In this world you are present in who you are and what you want while being fully, unapologetically you. Doesn't that sound epic?

That is called Bringing Your Big Energy!

Bringing Your Big Energy means aligning with your purpose, understanding what empowers you, and crafting an empowering plan to achieve your dreams. It's about embracing your core strengths, creating momentum, and illuminating your path to success. In this state you no longer need, or depend on, permission from others to live the life you want. You are the captain of your own boat and the writer of your own destiny.

This chapter is your personal invitation to ditch the approval-seeking game and grant yourself the ultimate freedom to embrace your quirks, flaws, and the beautifully messy parts that make you uniquely you. It's time to put aside the "should" and society's version of success to revel in the authenticity that comes from living on your terms. So buckle up and get ready to unleash the unapologetic, unfiltered version of yourself, because bringing your Big Energy is where the magic happens. Knowing and owning your voice and story is the way to get there.

Being authentic takes courage, guts, and vulnerability. It's not an easy path to choose. We need to embrace the willingness to expose our unique ideas, even if they are not shared by those around us. Bringing Your Big Energy means being open to sharing your imperfections and struggles from a place of curiosity and learning. When you're venturing into new territory, failure is not only a possibility but a probability with the ultimate aim of creating an authentic life and a journey you can truly be proud of!

When I think Big Energy, I think of April. April's journey has shaped her to be vulnerable, authentic, and unapologetic about her history, her story, and her struggles. Because of these struggles, and the discomfort of living authentically, she always felt like she was searching for a missing puzzle piece.

She finally found her true place, living her most authentic life, through getting back up again and again when she fell. On the other side of a challenging journey that required facing some drastic life-altering moments, she has found the freedom to fully know, own, and share her story.

For years, she chased the idea of a perfect life with a white picket fence, working hard to build it while constantly feeling like she wasn't enough. Now, having embraced her true self and reclaimed her narrative, April is an inspiration for those who follow behind her, showing them that struggles can lead to some of life's greatest achievements.

Her major Intensity Points began when she had to undergo several dental surgeries, leaving her with twenty-six pins in her jaw. She was in constant pain, which led to her doctor eventually prescribing her with Percocet.

During our conversation, she explains, "Percocet plugged in that missing piece that at the time I never realized I had, and I fell in love. Not because it cured my pain, but in my brain, I finally felt whole. It numbed everything else and completed me instead of me trying to complete myself."

With Percocet at her side, she was able to conquer everything from excelling at work, killing it as the PTA mom, and getting everything done in record time. She had found the answer she was looking for to keep up with and live the life that she yearned for. It was a dream come true until her dream became a nightmare.

Eventually, her prescribed doses were not enough, so she took more, and then more again, and an addiction was born. As her dependence on the drug escalated, her life spiraled out of control. Within a year, she lost her job, her children, her home, and the vehicle she lived in thereafter. She eventually ended up homeless.

What started as two pills a day became thirty, and what started as a prescribed medicine had turned into buying heroin on the streets. On the streets, she endured unspeakable experiences, eventually leading her to serving almost two years in prison—a fate that, in the end, she was thankful for because it was the only thing that could save her life. During her time within the walls of prison, she broke the chains of addiction and found her freedom. She discovered a deeper faith, forgave herself for her failures, and slowly began to love herself.

In the end, April's story is one of hope—finding a love of self and higher purpose to fill the void that material possessions and drugs never could. To this day, she shares her story freely and authentically as she advocates for heroin addicts and the homeless community. Her message is raw, honest, and real. We all stumble and learn that rising again often requires the support of others, lifting us up from our darkest days from a beautiful place of nonjudgment. She no longer fears being found out or being judged. She owns her previous membership in all of the communities she once was ashamed to be a part of. She stands strong, knowing her story and speaking her truth will help countless others. This currency is way more valuable than what others think about her.

She says, "I feel like this was exactly who I was supposed to be my whole life." Despite the struggles with drugs, April recognizes her journey was essential. Without it, she believes she would have remained unfulfilled and overwhelmed by anxiety. In the end, April feels profoundly blessed to have traveled along her complicated journey and to now fully embrace and own her story.

Being open to uncertainties transforms our ordinary stories into extraordinary journeys. Living authentically is not just a choice; it's a catalyst for living our best, most fulfilled life and a gateway to a more meaningful existence.

**VULNERABILITY**
You cannot celebrate and bring your authentic self, ignoring what others think, without vulnerability.

Brené Brown says, "Vulnerability is not winning or losing; it's having the courage to show up and be seen when we have no control over the outcome."[1]

She teaches that vulnerability is the cornerstone of human connection and personal growth. She underscores that it is not a sign of weakness but rather the birthplace of courage and authenticity.

Embracing vulnerability is critical for creating meaningful connections with people around us, fostering empathy, and living a full life. Through the willingness to be open, share our struggles, and engage with the world, we discover our strength and build deeper, more genuine relationships.

But like everything, it takes practice, so let's try one.

> **Ignite the Spark:** Find someone you trust—friend, family, close colleague, or coach—and choose a personal story that shows an aspect of yourself that you don't typically share. Share a personal experience with them where you faced fear and overcame it, a challenge you worked through, or a breakthrough in your self-discovery journey. Choose a moment that feels slightly uncomfortable but manageable, ensuring it doesn't cause unnecessary anxiety.
>
> Then take about five minutes to practice sharing it, letting your partner know what your goal is—for them to listen attentively without trying to fix, just holding a safe space for you. Once you have shared, ask your listener to respond with what they heard. When they

> do, work to be open to their thoughts, reactions, and support. While listening to them, pay attention to the emotions, thoughts, and whatever else comes up for you.
>
> After sharing, reflect on your experience. Ask yourself: "How did it feel to be vulnerable? What did I learn about myself and my connection with the listener? What came up for me mentally and physically during the session? How can I grow from this exercise?"

As you become more comfortable with vulnerability, consider sharing with others or exploring different aspects of your life. The goal is to gradually expand your comfort zone and build connections through openness.

Remember, vulnerability is a practice, and it's okay to start with smaller steps. Each time you share authentically, you strengthen your ability to connect with others on a deeper level and experience the transformative power of vulnerability. That's why practicing it over and over again is the key.

This may be hard at first, but I promise you—eventually, you will begin to grow in your comfort with it. Malcolm Gladwell's *Outliers* is a great guide to achieving mastery with practice. Gladwell found that people who are outliers, as defined by those who can achieve a mastery in their craft, have one big thing in common—ten thousand hours of focused practice. Putting in the work to practice your vulnerability is no different. Before long, you will be courageous in sharing in a more authentic way, feel lighter, and feel the alignment with your values and view like never before. As Gladwell says, "Practice isn't the thing you do once you're good. It's the thing you do that makes you good."[2]

I recently started working with Dan. Dan is a C-level executive in the technology space. He sought me out, through encouragement of the CEO, to work on softening his direct, and sometimes harsh, communication style so he could connect better with his peers and team. His manner of speaking caused a perception that he had little to no patience, snapping at people and emotionally reacting in negative ways.

During our introduction call, I dug in to gauge his level of awareness and readiness so I could evaluate my approach to the coaching that would resonate best with him. I sensed that the changes he would need to make would be incredibly challenging, given the well-worn path of his communication crutches. He had been operating in this way for decades, and changing his approach would take extensive commitment and energy. To be honest, I wasn't sure he was up for it. Being the coach I am, I lovingly told him that.

He acknowledged my concern, took a huge breath in, and assured me he was fully committed. Given what he had at stake, he was determined to make the change, no matter what it took. In that moment, I saw a rawness in his demeanor and body language. He was scared and somewhat desperate to improve; a lot was riding on our work together.

As we progressed, he shared that when he was perceived as being harsh, it was really him feeling emotionally triggered. His strong self-awareness indicated that his reactions were driven from his childhood environment and the effect it had on him. In being vulnerable with me, I was able to see a side of him that not one other single human being had ever seen (his words). He was terrified of losing his job, fearing becoming obsolete, struggling to meet expectations, and battling deep-seated imposter syndrome.

All of this was in spite of his C-level rank, recent promotion, and status as indispensable at the company.

Dan's story to me is a perfect one to showcase the importance of vulnerability. By opening up, I was able to see an entirely real side of him, where he felt safe to share openly about the hard season he was in. In sharing, he didn't know exactly how to fix it, but he knew he wanted to be better.

Having these elements were exactly the keys we needed to begin moving him into a learner's mindset mode, and his results were immediate. He was not the harsh, cold person people perceived him as but a beautiful, flawed, scared human. He had wanted to change his ways yet felt unsure where to start. Through our work together, given that we uncovered the root of the issue, he was able to begin making changes to his communication style and immediately noticed an increased connection with others.

So it matters. Vulnerability matters. Dan's story reminds us that vulnerability isn't a weakness. It's a bridge to transformation and growth.

## SELF-EXPRESSION

Let's talk a bit about practicing self-expression—another great way to unlock the doors to vulnerability and lead an authentic life. This involves sharing your thoughts, feelings, and opinions, even when it's hard. Courageous self-expression is about breaking free from societal expectations and allowing your true voice to be heard.

In a world that often encourages conformity, self-expression is a super powerful (and yes, I agree, scary) act of asserting your individuality and embracing authenticity. By expressing your thoughts, feelings, and unique perspectives, you grow as a person and also invite others to connect to you on a more intimate and genuine level. But sharing our true selves without masks or filters can be tough.

We live in a society where blending in has become the social norm. Take teenage girls, for example. As I sit here in 2024, when school lets out, the crowd is a sea of uniformity, all dressed in black leggings, oversized hoodies, crop tops, slippers, and carrying their forty-ounce water bottles. The conformity is undeniable!

So how do we practice breaking free from it? I especially see this professionally with my emerging leaders, those moving from senior managers into the director or executive suite where having and sharing your unique opinion is the key to climbing.

> **Ignite the Spark:** A powerful exercise is to deliberately formulate your opinion on something meaningful and practice sharing it. Expressing your opinion and

> embracing self-expression are closely intertwined. Start with a work-related topic you're responsible for and know well, and then practice articulating why it's important and how your unique perspective adds value to it. This not only strengthens your confidence in self-expression but also showcases your ability to contribute with authenticity and insight.
>
> Practice active listening to understand others' perspectives, and then respectfully express your own thoughts and opinions. Write it out and practice it. Then do a safe-to-fail experiment (introduced in chapter 6) and try it out. Share it in front of others. Be sure to express your point of view from a place of respect, root it in evidence, and remain open-minded. While at the same time, be clear about you own your belief and thoughtful about why you are offering it.
>
> As always, after practicing, reflect on what came up for you. Were you authentic? Could you feel self-doubt or self-monitoring creep in given the reaction of the group? Reflect in a curious, nonjudgmental way to see where you can continue to push yourself to experiment and grow in expressing yourself.

Gradually, as you become more comfortable articulating your ideas, you can explore opportunities to share your opinions in broader contexts.

Another way to think about and practice self-expression is through your artistic side. Even if you are not practicing it currently, I promise your power of creativity is there.

Finding another outlet can help you to express yourself in a more playful way without critiquing yourself. Use this safe space to explore yourself thoroughly through writing, journaling, painting, dancing, or anything that celebrates your uniqueness.

Embracing self-expression not only helps you grow as you shape the type of person or leader you want to be, but it also helps to foster understanding and empathy among diverse communities. As we honor the power of self-expression and embrace the rich mosaic of voices we are surrounded by, we begin to see how all of our individual stories come together—not in assimilation but in diversity. Essentially, if we don't bring our own voices to the table, the world will be more opaque, more conformist, and a heck of a lot less interesting.

**VALUE ALIGNMENT**

Mic is on a voyage to wake sleeping beauties, ignite female entrepreneur fires, pay it forward in life, and create an intense ripple effect of greatness by spreading support and kindness. All of these contributions ladder up to her purpose, which is making an impact on people and the world. I have never met someone quite like Mic, whose selfless nature is an inspiration for all.

I am humbled, impressed, and in awe with how aligned she is in the work she does and her values. Because of this incredible alignment, her energy is magnetic and contagious, whether connecting in person or through the inspirational words she shares virtually with her community.

Right now, she is focused on lifting women, but she has always had what she calls a "philanthropic heart," having been on both sides of the tables of life—the haves and the have nots. She learned it right from the beginning from her mom. Mic's mom modeled these values early and often, teaching Mic that there was always room at the table, always something to give. Whether they had a full pocket or only ten dollars left, her mom always found a way to help someone else.

Sometimes, they opened up their table to those who needed it most—giving them food and connection. Other times, they fell on hard times, and their community rose to pull up a chair at their respective tables. The aim was never to give with the expectation of receiving; instead, the universe and their great spirit simply provided them the chance to experience both.

In the work Mic does, she is creating space at the table for women to wake up and find their voices again. She is helping teach women the skills to speak their truth, to chase their dreams, and to tackle big dreams unapologetically. She loves nothing more than creating stages as she knows elevating these voices will make a huge difference in their lives and our world.

She just gets it. Square in her values, Mic shared, "At the end of my life, I have zero interest in talking about the handbags I have or the houses I have, or don't have, or my career. No, I want to know that people can raise a hand and say yeah, because of Mic, my life got better."

No additional exercise here, just remember your values and priorities we worked on in chapter 4. When you know and own your story, focusing on your values is critical to keep you anchored and centered on what matters most.

**BUILD CONFIDENCE**

I am an expert on imposter syndrome, which some say is the opposite of being confident. I am an expert not only because I teach classes on it but because I consistently fall into old patterns where I let myself believe I am not good enough. Sometimes I tackle it quickly and never look back, and sometimes it lingers. Sometimes it shows up when I least expect it, but it always creates a shadow over my confidence.

For almost thirteen years at Google, I thought I would be found out, that I didn't belong, that my pedigree and world-traveling experiences were not on par with many of my Harvard and McKinsey peers. Ironically, when researching this book, it crept back in. As I researched my topic category, I found mountains of amazing writing that already existed on these topics. At one point, I became so despondent I almost gave up. I was unsure I would be able to produce anything unique or worth sharing in the sea of experts.

These days I am getting better at catching myself, and I was able to reframe my thinking. Instead of "It's already been done," I let myself appreciate other people's existing work as "Validation that the conversation is out there, and I need to be a part of it." I reminded myself that the voice and stories I am bringing to my readers are unique and add valuable perspective. By reframing the narrative in my head, I was able to see the real evidence that exists. I was able to take away the power of my imposter syndrome and move into a healthier view that served me—getting this book out there to help you!

*Psychology Today* says those who struggle with imposter syndrome believe they are undeserving of their achievements and the high esteem in which they are, in fact, generally held. They feel they aren't as competent or intelligent as others might think and that soon enough, people will discover the truth about them. Those with imposter syndrome, which is not an official diagnosis, are often well-accomplished; they may hold high office or have numerous academic degrees.

As a result, you over-credit the work and skills of others, are paralyzed by fear of failure, and are driven by perfectionism while suffering from self-doubt the entire time. This mindset undermines confidence and hinders individuals from recognizing and celebrating their successes. Imposter syndrome leads to negative self-talk, which can erode self-esteem and contribute to feelings of inadequacy, holding you back from discovering what else could be possible.[3]

Research shows that 70 percent of people will suffer from it at one point in their life.[4] Imposter syndrome also tends to be more common in women and underrepresented communities, with an estimated 75 percent of women compared to 40 percent of men.[5]

Most imposter syndrome can be linked back to our story of origin. These are the big assumptions we hold to be true about ourselves and what we are capable of. The key to increasing confidence is rewiring these stories.

My story? I was a townie. I grew up in a resort town, and every year, the summer people—who we called the fudgies because they headed north for vacation and fudge—appeared in town decked out in their spiffy new summer clothes with their fancy cars, tennis whites, and perfect tans. I waited tables and scooped ice cream each year to these summer people who had all the pedigrees and not a care in the world. I never felt enough; at worst, they were rude to me as the hired help, and at best, they found me invisible.

So fast forward twenty years later when I joined Google. I had packed up that story nicely, despite almost fifteen years of work experience, and carried it right along with me into the best company on earth. On day one, we had a bonding activity, and in true Google fashion, we began with icebreakers. Where do you summer? Where did you study abroad? What alma mater did you hail from? And so on. I felt so small. It was the summer fudgies all over again, which meant I had to keep my townie hidden. I am embarrassed to say that I never quite worked it out for myself during the thirteen years I was at Google.

Instead, I overcompensated by taking on more, traveling more, getting that next promotion, until I broke down. Now I know how dangerous these stories are, and they are just that—stories. As I've grown, I've learned that countering these stories with rational thought, factual evidence, and positive affirmations diminishes their power and frees you from their influence. When we do this we are able to let the confidence bloom in its place.

It can show up anywhere. I interviewed Derek because he went from being a chemist to a dentist at age forty, making a major career shift that I think is super brave and interesting. Yet during our interview he admitted: "I was not exactly filled with confidence." He went on to talk about how his mentor "exuded confidence."

It was not until he had the support of his mentor challenging him and believing in him while he also continued to develop new skills that he finally felt like he had "arrived." This man held a PhD in organic chemistry from Yale and had worked as a chemist at a leading pharmaceutical company, yet even he struggled with imposter syndrome as he transitioned from a familiar career into one where he lacked experience. Nonetheless, he bravely challenged himself to work through it.

So what can we do about it? I believe we can do three key things to increase our confidence.

To start, we need to break down the walls of denial and avoidance, and the best way to do that is through radical acceptance. Tara Brach, PhD, psychologist, author of *Radical Acceptance: Embracing Your Life with the Heart of a Buddha*, and expert on Buddhist meditation, teaches that radical acceptance means practicing a conscious effort to acknowledge and honor difficult situations and emotions. By fully accepting our situation—instead of ignoring, avoiding, or wishing it were different—we create the space to move from where we are to where we want to be.[6]

> **Ignite the Spark:** One powerful way to engage in radical acceptance is through journaling. Set aside time where you can be alone with your thoughts and begin by writing about your current experiences, focusing on the challenges you're facing and the emotions that come up for you. Approach this exercise with curiosity, exploring your feelings without judgment. Capture how these emotions affect your life, relationships, and well-being. Reflect on any resistance you feel. Why is it there? What are you afraid to confront?

As you continue, gently consider how accepting these emotions might change your perspective. Consider the possibility that acknowledging and embracing your reality, despite it being uncomfortable, could be the key to unlocking your growth and healing. Let your thoughts flow freely, knowing you aren't trying to solve everything at once but taking the first step toward embracing and accepting yourself exactly how you are.

A second step is challenging the stories we are telling ourselves. This is all about challenging the assumptions we have about ourselves and our abilities. Assumptions are ideals we hold tightly to and things that we believe to be true. I see these showing up as stories, much like mine I shared before. What stories are we telling ourselves, and what is actually true about them?

> **Ignite the Spark:** You can test these stories through simple journaling, in which you ask yourself these four questions: What stories am I telling myself? What is

> true about them? Can I reframe them? And my favorite question: What else could be true?

Evidence gathering is another way to challenge your stories. By writing down a brag sheet, starting each sentence with "I know that I can ____" provides the evidence you need to tear down the walls of your stories and replace them with reality-based insights instead.

Lastly, this one doesn't get talked about enough, but I truly believe in some cases we are experiencing imposter syndrome because we are trying to be something we are not. Because our strengths and capabilities are not congruent with the system and/or environment we are in. Put simply, we are trying to fit in and are comparing ourselves to others.

Teddy Roosevelt and others were right when they said, "Comparison is the thief of joy."[7]

By continuously comparing ourselves to others, we chip away at our confidence, get in our own way, and feed the imposter syndrome monster. This is especially dangerous when we are comparing someone's finished product to where we are starting. It is like a third grader comparing his short story with his freshman sister's. Hers will absolutely be better. She's obtained more experience, learned more lessons, and is likely hundreds of hours closer to the ten thousand hours of practice.

To stop comparing yourself to others, it all starts with self-awareness and embracing your unique journey. It is about realizing that we all have our own path, strengths, and voice.

You can also let go of comparison through setting goals that align with your values and aspirations, and measure your progress based on your own standards, not external benchmarks. See, full circle—back to our calling our own personal success shot.

Gradually shifting your mindset toward self-acceptance and appreciation and recognizing that your journey is uniquely yours and worthy of celebration will be one of the best gifts you can give yourself. Remember that you are unique, beautiful, and talented and all your own ways—and exactly perfect how you are today.

**KNOW AND OWN YOUR STORY**

Owning your story means embracing your life experiences, including the challenges and successes, and allowing them to shape who you are without letting them define you completely.

Prior to writing this book, I did not own my story—at least not fully and consistently. It took almost five months from the book's inception for me to have the guts and courage to post about this book on LinkedIn. Five months! I was worried that my story would be seen as pitiful, too dramatic, or too vulnerable.

But then one day I decided to own it and share it. And then I held my breath and crawled under the covers with my teen, and guess what! Fifteen thousand people were exposed, connected, and engaged with my post in less than twenty-four hours. Why? Because people connected with my story. It made them feel something and provided them with value.

Likely, sharing my story reminded them that they are not alone in whatever challenges they are tackling, because the truth is, as much as we are all different, our struggles are often the same.

Seeing my community rise up to show interest and love for what I have to share was the most incredible feeling in the world and, in fact, completely the opposite of my fear. Instead of weakness, they saw bravery and realness that is not shared often enough. Comment after comment rolled in on my social outreach. Collectively, they were all validating that the world needs more open sharing and more of these stories of trying, falling, and getting back up again. People are starving for the true stories that remind them they are not out there on their own facing the forces of the world on their own.

Sharing and owning your story is terrifying and empowering all at the same time, but absolutely a must-do if you want to unlock the authentic you!

Your story is not a collection of trivial moments; it's a patchwork quilt of things you've learned, threads of your experiences, challenging war wounds, and triumphant champagne bubbles. It's a narrative uniquely yours, filled with chapters of resilience, growth, and transformation.

When you share and own your stories, you invite others into the beauty and complexity of your journey, sharing and engaging in experiences and helping them to embrace their own story with energy and courage. Each chapter you share comes with the power to uplift, connect, and heal yourself and others. Our stories are not meant to be lived and then hidden. They are meant to celebrate—the good, the bad, and the ugly—as proof of our resilience and an inspiration of what is possible to us and others.

> **Ignite the Spark:** A powerful way to remember, uncover, and know your full story is by creating something called a lifeline. A lifeline is a visual timeline spanning from birth to the present, marking significant events and milestones—both positive and negative—such as graduations, job changes, relationships, challenges, and achievements. To truly capture your story, shape the line with peaks and valleys that mirror the highs and lows of your energy throughout each season of your life. This exercise helps you reflect on your personal growth and the key moments that have shaped you.

These events and the lessons you've learned are valuable nuggets to leverage as you craft the story you want to tell about yourself and your life. It is key to also reflect after you complete the exercise, best if with a friend or a coach, to explore what you've learned, themes, and insights that emerge.

Developing your own personal branding statement, also sometimes called an elevator pitch, is an effective way to create and practice your story.[8]

Crafting your own personal branding statement is all about sharing—in a short, sweet, and powerful way—who you are, what you stand for, and what makes you unique. It's a way to let the world know what you bring to the table and why you matter. By articulating your personal brand, you not only define your personal and/or professional identity but also magnetize energy for opportunities that align with your goals. It helps you to articulate what you want, stand out, let people know what you care about, and cut through all the noise.

And it should be short! The amount of time it takes you for an elevator ride is why these are sometimes called an elevator pitch. Princeton University says an elevator pitch is a brief, think thirty seconds, way of introducing yourself, getting across a key point or two, and making a connection with someone.[9]

Questions to ask yourself when crafting this are: What do you stand for? What do you want people to leave thinking about you or feeling about you? What are your core values and beliefs? What are your key strengths, skills, and areas of expertise that set you apart? What qualities or characteristics do others consistently recognize and appreciate in you? What words or phrases best capture the essence of who you are and what you stand for personally? Professionally?

Here is an example personal branding statement: I am a leadership coach with over twenty-five years of experience helping executives and teams unlock their potential. Through a blend of strategic insight and personalized guidance, I empower clients to overcome challenges, enhance their skills, and achieve their goals with authenticity and growth.

Capture these notes and then practice delivering your pitch to people in your Energy Hype Squad.

Let me show how powerful this can be.

Laura was working with me to secure a new position. She had grown up at her current company for the first ten years of her career, and although she was excited for her next chapter, she was really struggling with how to tell her story. We spent a lot of time together crafting her personal brand statement, and one day she had an amazing breakthrough.

The key? She had been introducing herself from the vantage point of all the things she could expertly do in her current role. It was all true. She was talented, had a wealth of knowledge, and was extremely capable. When she practiced it on me, however, it just felt flat.

In my role, as the perspective interviewer in our role play, I did not see her as memorable. I was not convinced she was passionate about coming to work for me at my nonprofit, and through the use of all her industry buzzwords, I was lost on "why her."

So I started to probe her: What did she like about the work she was doing? Why did it matter? In the end, what drove her? And on her breakthrough day, it popped when she told me, "I care about social injustice. I care about providing access to skills and training for marginalized groups to enable them to secure a better life for themselves."

And there it was—her story. As a marginalized person herself, having walked that journey and now having the ability to give this opportunity to others was her life's work. That was what mattered to her. That was the "why" of her story. Everything else was just the how. From then on out, Laura used her new empowered passionate personal brand statement and, in the end, finally was able to secure her dream leadership role at a nonprofit active in serving children in marginalized communities locally.

Ultimately, knowing and sharing your story is all about being true to yourself—embracing and sharing your individuality, values, and beliefs. It's about allowing yourself to be vulnerable, practicing self-expression, and aligning your actions with your deepest values to own a story that is uniquely yours. When your life harmonizes with your core principles, you experience a profound sense of fulfillment, like finding the perfect puzzle piece that completes the bigger picture of who you are. This alignment optimizes your life, empowering you to make decisions that resonate with your truest self and live at your best energy currency.

Believe in yourself and bring that full version of yourself—your Big Energy—because not a single soul on this planet can bring your same perspective and energy. Let it shine!

CHAPTER 8

# BRING YOUR BIG "LEADER" ENERGY

---

*"Good leaders must communicate vision clearly, creatively, and continually. However, the vision doesn't come alive until the leader models it."*

—JOHN C. MAXWELL

**IGNITE YOUR LEADERSHIP**

The goal of this chapter is to explore how you can implement the SPARK process as a leader. Now that you have a stronger understanding of your personal and professional self, we'll delve into how you can authentically integrate that into the leader you aspire to be and how you present yourself. Beyond your own growth, this chapter will also guide you on how to align your team with the same powerful, kinetic energy, helping everyone thrive together.

Although this chapter focuses on team leadership, remember that leadership isn't tied to a specific title or level. No matter your role, you can skillfully apply the SPARK process to shape your team's culture and drive best-in-class results.

Leadership is crucial for building high-performing teams, and when it's lacking, it can become a leading factor in poor employee retention. People don't quit jobs. They quit managers and leaders. A study by Development Dimensions International, a global leadership consulting firm, found that 57 percent of employees have left jobs due to frustration with their manager or company leadership.[1]

With nearly three decades of experience in corporate leadership, and coaching hundreds of emerging and senior leaders, I'm uniquely positioned to share key strategies for elevating your leadership. Integrating SPARK into your approach will empower you to lead with intention, effectiveness, and authenticity while fostering a team environment built on trust, clarity, and shared purpose.

**WHAT LEADERS NEED TO BE SUCCESSFUL**

Leaders face the dual challenge and opportunity of guiding their teams through change and uncertainty. They're expected to identify problems, provide solutions, and inspire progress despite the chaos. But leadership doesn't happen in isolation. Leaders collectively achieve results through building and nurturing their teams.

As I mentioned earlier in the book, I pursued coaching because I wanted to make a greater impact by helping people unlock their passions, goals, dreams, and visions.

As a coach, I've stepped back from my formal leadership role to empower others to lead. I leverage my expertise to help leaders develop deeper self-awareness and cultivate genuine, trusted influence with their teams.

Coaching leaders holds special significance for me because they are often overlooked when it comes to personal development. As leaders rise higher, they can find themselves increasingly isolated, making it harder to ask questions or embrace a learner's mindset. They are expected to know all of the answers. Despite many courses on management and operationalizing teams, there's a gap in coaching individuals on becoming inspirational, motivational leaders while remaining authentic.

When leaders lead with purpose and authenticity, they foster trust and commitment, motivating their teams to unite behind a common goal. This kind of inspiration not only boosts performance and innovation but also creates a positive, cohesive culture where individuals feel valued and empowered. Inspired followers are more likely to go above and beyond, contributing to long-term success and a shared sense of achievement.

The good news is that everything we've covered with SPARK is designed to help you lead authentically and bring the Big Energy your team craves and deserves.

In this chapter, I've included the key elements of great leadership and team building, considerations to keep in mind, exercises to try, expected outcomes, and examples to clarify each concept.

**SELF-REFLECTION**
Back in chapter 3, we underwent some pretty hefty self-reflection together. Through this work, you were able to reflect more through looking inward, finding peace, and listening to yourself to uncover clarity. We also addressed how to leverage our decision-making skills to find solutions for our future and underwent an energy assessment to identify our ignitors and drainers.

Each of these lessons equips you to stand confidently in your true self and offers insights on how to incorporate that into your leadership role. You did all this great work, which is essential and will empower you to bring your full self to success as a leader.

So with that being said, let's start by assessing where you see yourself as a leader.

**LEADERSHIP SELF-ASSESSMENT**
This exercise helps you clarify your leadership style, recognize strengths and challenges, and chart a growth path. It's a tool to explore your ongoing leadership journey, emphasizing reflection and adaptation for lasting improvement. By assessing your challenges and applying your strengths, you can uncover solutions and opportunities for enrichment.

> **Ignite the Spark:** Start by reflecting on your leadership role and evaluating where you stand—particularly the challenges you face.
>
> To organize your thoughts, on a piece of paper create three columns. Label the first column "Current Challenges," the second "Strengths I Can Leverage," and the third "What I Need to Do Differently." This framework allows you to break down your challenges and identify strengths you can harness to address them.

For example, if you feel overwhelmed by your workload, and lack time for strategic thinking, you would write "overwhelmed" in the "Current Challenges" column. Then, in the "Strengths I Can Leverage" column, you might note the strong critical thinking skills you possess and highlight your supportive capable leadership team. In the "What I Need to Do Differently" column, you will reflect on actionable steps that you can take through trying some different approaches.

Given that "What I Need to Do Differently" will be how you align "Current Challenges" and "Strengths I Can Leverage," this is where you will spend the bulk of your time. You will establish your solutions through trying things a bit differently to encourage the change you hope to see in this area.

Once you've identified these solutions, through applying your strengths, create an action plan for "What I Need to Do Differently." Breaking your solutions into actionable steps will ensure that you're addressing challenges while fostering growth.

In our example above, "What I Need to Do Differently" could be an action such as "delegating more effectively." With your challenge of being overwhelmed, and too busy to focus on big-picture thinking, you will apply your strengths of critical thinking and operational efficiency to begin delegating more effectively. Delegating will not only free up your time but also empower your team and foster their growth.

Through a personal reflection process, some effective questions you may ask yourself are:

- Why am I not delegating more? What is getting in my way?
- What needs to happen for me to trust my team to take full ownership of their projects?
- What tasks and projects are the highest and best use of my time?
- What can I do differently to assure I am prioritizing my strategic time?

It is important to note here in our delegation example that doing the hard things—like strategic thinking or solving more ambiguous problems—can be incredibly challenging. It is much easier for us to reach for the easier tasks that we can do with our eyes closed because they usually are etched in well-worn patterns. However, when we get caught up in busy work, entire days slip away. While it feels good to accomplish tasks, we're not advancing or focusing on the leadership work we're uniquely positioned to do within the team.

In our example, a tactical action step may be to assure we are blocking out strategic time and protecting it. To assure the best use of honoring that time, I would recommend setting aside some preplanning time to get goals around what strategic thinking will look like, booking yourself a conference room with a whiteboard or your version of changing scenery and encouraging creative space, and avoiding any and all distractions to assure focus.

On a daily basis, outside of your protected time, each time you're tempted to take on a task, ask yourself if it's an opportunity for someone on your team to develop. Similarly, assess your meeting schedule to see if delegating your attendance could free up time for strategic thinking while offering growth opportunities to others.

As with anything, it will be important to assess how you will know if you are being more strategic. What will be your sign? How can you assure you are not falling into old patterns?

So, hopefully, this is a helpful way to align your strengths to overcome challenges and push on your learning edges to grow as a leader.

One last thing to note as you undergo your leadership assessment—and I cannot stress enough—is the importance of authenticity in leadership and making sure your personal values and your leadership style are consistently aligned. It's essential to integrate what you value as a person into your leadership style. For example, if integrity is one of your core values, how are you incorporating that into how you lead? Remember, when you lead with authenticity, you not only stay true to yourself, but you also inspire and empower those around you to do the same. Your leadership becomes a force that drives real, meaningful change.

During my first decade as a leader at Google, I led with heart. I guided my teams to consistently overachieve by focusing on solid strategies while prioritizing everyone as individuals. I brought compassion into my leadership and took the time to understand what drove each team member and what truly mattered to them.

However, later in my career, I found myself in a role that required a data-first approach, with little opportunity to be a heart first leader. This shift led to heightened anxiety and exacerbated my imposter syndrome. I no longer focused on getting to know the whole person, and my leadership became more about the numbers than fostering a shared human goal. As a result, my team became less inspired and began to lose that collective sense of purpose that magically bonded us and drove us to succeed together.

## TEAM SELF-ASSESSMENT

Now that you've reflected on your personal leadership strengths, it's time to think about how to bring that clarity to your team.

> **Ignite the Spark:** Start by having your team members engage in their own self-reflection as prework before your team session. Encourage them to revisit chapter 3 in this book, focusing on how they see themselves and their vision for the team. If the book isn't available to

> everyone, provide a summary or key points to guide their reflection.
>
> Next, you will come together to reflect on and discuss past experiments, both successful and detrimental, and assess team culture, dynamics, and strategy effectiveness.

This process is helping your team understand the current state of affairs of themselves and the group, identifying what's working and what isn't. This reflection encourages open communication, accountability, and a mindset of continuous improvement. It helps in setting clear, actionable goals, aligning everyone's efforts toward a shared purpose, and building on successes while learning from failures.

As you did in the "Self-Reflection" chapter, the best way to assess energy levels is through the "Igniters and Drainers" model. Gather your team, either in person or virtually, and use a whiteboard or online collaborative platform to set the tone. Make it clear that this is a forward-looking session, not a venting event.

The goal is to identify what the energy on the team looks like and pinpoint areas for improvement before diving into values and purpose work. Start by exploring questions together like:

1. What's energizing us?
2. Why does it ignite our energy?
3. What would be the ideal energy flow?
4. What's draining our energy?
5. Where do these energy drainers show up?

6. How can we channel our energy more effectively?
7. What steps will we take to boost our energy and reduce drains?

I once conducted this energy assessment with my team at Google, and the impact on the team's health and well-being was unforgettable. After doing this work, and despite all the energy we were putting in, we discovered how overwhelmed we felt; we were only spinning our wheels without making progress.

Through this workshop, we developed actionable solutions such as consolidating meetings, handling tasks via email instead of meeting, establishing a more effective way to keep each other informed to avoid parallel pathing, and other inefficiencies that were draining our energy. By addressing these, we were able to streamline our processes and improve overall morale.

As you round out this process, consider the connection between self, leadership, team dynamics, and authenticity. Reflect on how each element interrelates, leveraging the insights from the rest of the chapter. Remember that leading authentically not only enhances your personal growth but also strengthens the bond within your team, creating a more cohesive and effective group committed to shared goals.

**PURPOSE**

Having established a strong foundation with your personal leadership traits, values, and purpose, it's now time to extend this understanding to your team through creating a shared vision and values.

Guiding your team through a values exercise is a powerful way to build alignment and foster a shared sense of purpose. Begin with the executive level and then engage their direct reports to ensure strong buy-in by tapping into their insights on the business and team dynamics.

> **Ignite the Spark:** Begin by identifying core values through discussions that highlight personal stories and experiences. The team must first clarify their purpose—defining the work they exist to accomplish together.

Depending on team size, work as a whole group or in small breakout sessions to address these key questions:

- Which values have shaped our identity and driven our success up to this point?
- What core values influence our interactions with each other, our customers, and our employees?
- How do we want our team to be remembered? What actions and achievements will define our legacy?

If working in small groups, reconvene to share findings. Then, as a whole team, use a whiteboard to discuss: "To fulfill our team's purpose, what values need to govern our decisions and actions?"

Then, have each team member independently write down ten values they believe are crucial to the team's success, ranking each by importance. Once they have each completed the exercise, work collaboratively to fine-tune the collective list to create one shared values list. Continue the dialogue through ranking and trimming until the team agrees on five to seven core values.

- Depending on team size and dynamics, this process can take anywhere from a couple of hours to a full day or more.
- Multiple iterations may be necessary, so adapt the process as needed.

Finally, craft a shared purpose statement that encapsulates these values and serves as a guiding beacon for the entire organization. This vision should be concise, inspiring, and reflective of the team's collective aspirations. Use it as a filter for decision-making, ensuring alignment and consistency in pursuing goals. The goal is to unite your team around shared ambitions and clarify your collective "why."

A strong purpose statement should clearly articulate the team's mission, inspire and motivate its members, and emphasize the positive impact they aim to create. It should align with core values, promote collaboration and inclusivity, and include a vision for the future. Concise and memorable, it serves as a guiding force that unites the team and drives their actions.

A strong purpose statement for a team could look like:

"Our purpose is to innovate and deliver exceptional solutions that empower our clients to achieve their goals. We are committed to fostering a collaborative, inclusive environment where every team member is valued and inspired to contribute their best, driving us to exceed expectations and create meaningful impact in everything we do."

By integrating these values along with a purpose statement into daily operations, you foster a cohesive and motivated team driven by a common purpose. This approach promotes transparency, collaboration, and engagement, empowering leaders to guide their teams toward achieving best-in-class results.

Angie, a standout leader on my management team at Google, excelled in team vision setting. When stepping into a new role, she had a remarkable ability to establish clear expectations and create a compelling team vision and purpose. Angie brought a unique twist to this process by embedding the concept of ownership into her leadership approach. She didn't just see her team as employees; she saw them as owners of a multimillion-dollar company.

This mindset shift changed everything. Ownership drove solutions instead of problems and fostered leaders rather than just players.

To solidify this sense of ownership, Angie had her teams identify their most aspirational brands and explain why. The exercise generated a bank of words that later became the foundation for naming their "business" and defining their purpose. This process gave the team a sense of ownership in crafting their new business identity, setting the tone for how they wanted to be perceived and what they stood for.

From there, Angie and her leadership team aligned the newly defined purpose with business metrics to pinpoint strengths, weaknesses, and growth opportunities. This laid the groundwork for a focused and streamlined business strategy. Each team member took on a specific role as a board member, responsible for a key strategic area. Team meetings transformed into board meetings with each member reporting on their area of ownership.

At the end of each quarter, the team conducted an audit of their strategy to track progress and identify areas for adjustment. This approach not only created a high-performance team but also fostered a strong bond among its members.

Angie's teams were consistently high-performing and deeply loyal, with many members returning to work with her two or three times over the years. Her consistently positive upward feedback and success as a leader underscore the power of setting a clear vision and purpose and using creativity to make it uniquely your own.

### ABANDON

Once your vision is clear, it's vital to remove distractions that don't align with your shared goals and values. This allows you to focus on the scope and impact you're meant to create. Anything outside this scope should be reassigned or removed. As a leader, recognize that taking on extraneous tasks can dilute your team's focus and efficiency.

> **Ignite the Spark:** Encourage regular evaluations of workloads to identify tasks that don't contribute to the

vision. Use the self-reflection work you did earlier to identify issues, then "clean house" to remove distractions. Some questions to ask the team are:

- What do we need to unplug that is draining our energy?
- What activities can we ignite that fuel our passion and drive?
- What processes or practices do we need to rewire to enhance our success?

By systematically eliminating distractions, you free up time and energy to focus on what truly matters. This approach not only boosts productivity but also empowers team members, providing them with clarity and purpose. It enables everyone to channel their efforts toward high-impact activities that drive progress and innovation. Cultivating a culture of strategic prioritization ensures that every action and initiative is purposeful and aligned with overarching goals. Thus, removing nonessential tasks becomes a powerful strategy for helping your team reach its full potential and achieve deserved success.

Here are some examples of implementing unplug, ignite, and rewire:

- **Unplug:** Eliminate practices that drain energy, such as an excessive number of meetings or redundant processes.
- **Ignite:** Foster activities that energize and inspire the team, such as innovative projects or recognition initiatives.
- **Rewire:** Adjust or replace ineffective practices with new approaches that enhance team effectiveness.

## RESULTS

As emphasized earlier, having a clear and compelling vision is crucial. Through this abandon practice, it is often helpful to choose and concentrate on three to five key pillars or goals for your team. Any more than this can lead to dilution of focus. The clearer the "why" and the results needed, the more inspirational and enjoyable the journey toward success will be.

To align with your values and vision, brainstorm and identify the key pillars essential for achieving your goals. Engage in open discussion to determine:

- What are the critical pillars we need to adopt to make our values and vision a reality?
- What working norms and team principles should we establish to ensure effective collaboration?

Examples of high-performing team pillars:

- Consistency: Ensures reliable performance and builds trust by providing a stable and predictable environment for team members.
- Trust: Fosters open communication and collaboration, enabling team members to feel safe sharing ideas and taking risks.
- Accountability: Encourages personal responsibility and commitment, ensuring everyone contributes to team goals and takes ownership of their actions.
- Psychological safety: Creates a supportive atmosphere where team members feel comfortable expressing

themselves without fear of judgment, leading to greater innovation and engagement.

As a leader, embody these principles and lead by example. Transition from merely speaking about values to actively demonstrating them through your actions. This alignment between words and actions enhances credibility and reinforces the commitment to the shared vision.

By filtering out distractions and focusing on key priorities, your team will experience increased clarity, motivation, and cohesion. This strategic approach fosters a productive and empowered environment where everyone is aligned and driven toward achieving exceptional results.

**KINETIC ENERGY**

Let's unify our approach through the kinetic energy step introduced in chapter 7. In the context of a team, kinetic energy embodies the dynamic and ever-evolving force that propels your team's identity and growth. Just as kinetic energy represents the energy of motion in physics, in a team setting, it symbolizes the vibrant and continuous momentum generated when your team's purpose, goals, and core pillars are aligned.

This energy thrives through authentic engagement and embraces the ongoing changes within the team, driving progress and boosting overall effectiveness. By harnessing this kinetic energy, your team can excel, adapt, and achieve its collective goals with renewed enthusiasm and unity.

Building team cohesiveness is a key step in this, and in creating it, you are fostering unity, trust, and collaboration among members. Strong, cohesive teams are more effective, innovative, and resilient. Leaders who focus on team cohesiveness enhance communication, morale, and collective success by leveraging the diverse strengths of their team.

In the spirit of offering you a taste of what this could look like, I have sketched out what a one-hour meeting could look like to start pulling together team cohesiveness.

Example one-hour agenda:

- Set the tone: Begin with the leader creating a safe environment for open discussion and engagement.
- Review the SPARK process: Recap the SPARK process, focusing on integrating purpose, goals, and core pillars.
- Kinetic energy exercise: Assess current team dynamics and identify elements that are either draining energy or igniting it.
- Action plan: Develop strategies to unplug distractions, amplify energy sources, and rewire areas for improvement.
- Group discussion: Facilitate a conversation on how to align team actions with the collective vision and values.
- Commitment and next steps: Outline actionable steps and assign responsibilities to ensure sustained momentum and cohesion.

Effective team dialogue hinges on asking the right questions that inspire reflection, spark energy, and foster a shared sense of purpose.

> **Ignite the Spark:** To drive meaningful conversations and align your team toward a common goal, consider these ten powerful questions that encourage openness, exploration, and collective growth.
>
> 1. What do you want to achieve as a team?
> 2. What strengths do you have that can help you reach your goals?
> 3. What challenges might you face in pursuing these goals?
> 4. What emerging story is unfolding within the team?
> 5. What is the collective voice of the team beyond individual perspectives?
> 6. What dream are we striving toward?
> 7. What possibilities excite you about this journey?
> 8. How can we reframe challenges as opportunities?
> 9. What can we learn from others in our field?
> 10. How does the current climate impact our vision and objective?

After experiencing the impact of our one-hour session, I am confident you'll recognize the value of investing more time to deepen these strategies. Imagine what your team could accomplish with a full day dedicated to immersive leadership development.

My business partner and I offer full-day coaching sessions that build on the initial work. These sessions include hands-on learning, personalized guidance, and collaborative exercises to strengthen trust and cohesion. These workshops provide the opportunity to refine leadership skills while addressing individual and team needs in a supportive, focused setting.

In our full-day team events, participants:

- Engage in immersive leadership development with hands-on learning elements.
- Cultivate cohesiveness and trust through collaborative activities and exercises.
- Enhance leadership skills to navigate complex issues with confidence.
- Receive tailored advisory support to address individual needs and goals.
- Develop emotional intelligence for more effective communication and relationship-building.
- Boost confidence and career satisfaction through personal growth initiatives.

By focusing on these elements, you can bring all the pieces together to create a high-energy, cohesive, and well-performing team. This sets the stage for transforming your team's dynamics in a trusting, fun, and safe environment.

Jordan, a team leader at a marketing agency, was struggling with low team morale and inefficiency due to long, unproductive meetings and redundant tasks. After implementing a one-hour Kinetic Energy session, the team identified and eliminated energy-draining activities, focused on what invigorated them, and restructured their processes to be more collaborative and efficient. As a result, meetings became more productive, team engagement increased, and overall morale improved, leading to enhanced creativity and effectiveness.

Lastly, here are a few reflections from participants who have experienced meaningful changes through our team coaching programs:

- "This is a powerful program for any professional seeking to move forward in their careers. The group sessions and one-on-one advisory provided great information and actionable items."
- "The executive coaching program has been an invaluable experience. We tackled real-time challenges and identified areas for personal development. I can't thank the coaches enough for their time and help in my personal and professional life."
- "This experience was awesome. Our coaches are a great duo, and I appreciate the warm environment that allows others, and me, to open up."
- "The overall coaching program was transformative. The structured sessions, combined with insightful guidance, significantly enhanced my skills and confidence. The supportive environment fostered growth and collaboration, making it an invaluable experience. Highly recommend!"

Regardless of where you are in your leadership journey, leveraging the SPARK process and focusing on your continuous development is essential to empower you to not only grow but to model a culture of growth, adaptability, and resilience.

While not comprehensive, focusing on some of the areas I highlighted above will equip you with the essential skills needed to inspire your teams, drive innovation, and achieve sustained success.

To further accelerate your progress and enhance team cohesion, consider joining our immersive team workshop, where we provide hands-on strategies and personalized support to help you unlock your team's full potential.

## CHAPTER 9

# EMBRACE YOUR EPIC ENERGY

---

"*The journey of a thousand miles begins with one step.*"
—LAO TZU

"*Sometimes when you're in a dark place, you think you've been buried, but actually you've been planted. Struggle makes you grow.*"
—CHRISTINE CAINE

**THIS TIME**

In 2024, just months before this book enters production, I will lose both my breasts. It feels surreal to face this challenge while at the same time sharing these tools and experiences with you, helping you transform hard moments into fuel for what comes next. The parallel is not lost on me.

I would be lying if I said I was not terrified. Heading back into battle this time has the triggers of what came before and the fear of the unknown—since it is both a more aggressive cancer and treatment this time. I feel like I am living outside of my body, but I have learned along the way that it's just because I have never experienced this exact season before, so I give myself grace.

I believe this all is happening for a reason, though. I have to believe that in my forty-ninth year, there is still a greater plan for what lies ahead, and not all my new experiences and joy are behind me.

I press on because I know in my heart I need to be there for my girls, my family, and my friends, and I need to inspire others to keep moving—one step in front of the other.

In the spirit of processing and sharing authentically, I want to offer this:

This time I am doing it different.
This time I am not hiding in shame.
This time I am putting it out there.
This time I am being me.
This time I am telling the truth.
This time I do not soldier on alone.

I have breast cancer.

Again.

I am praying for the best-case scenario.

I am crushed by the guilt that I survived the first time.
I am terrified of the process, and I know it is going to be more aggressive than last time.
I am terrified it is everywhere, the fear is real.

This time I ask for help.
This time I ask for hugs.
This time I tell the story.
This time I pray I can help others do the same.

I am unaware why I am here again.
I am unsure why the Lord is offering up this Intensity Point for me.
Yet I know there must be a reason.

I have so much to live for.
My girls.
My parents.
My husband.
My doggie.
My beautiful business partners and clients.

Please do not pity me.
Please do not treat me differently.
Please still assume I am the same old me.
Please give me connection, the last time was so incredibly lonely.

This time I grow again, learn again, and pray to help others do the same.
This time I survive, again.
This time I bring my Big "Pink" Energy.

I share this with you now because it's authentically me and a part of my journey. The days are up and down between tears, appointments, conversations, and worrying.

Yet at the same time, in real time, it occurs to me that I have more at my disposal this time. I will leverage my SPARK process to pave my path of transformation moving forward. I will spend time in self-reflection, identifying what I learned from my past experience and what I want to do differently. I will spend time thinking deeply about the purpose of this happening not to me but for me and making sure I leverage all of it to help others.

I have already started to abandon the shame, guilt, and the shoulds so I can focus on what is going to serve me most each day along the way. In terms of results, I am focusing on my biggest goal on getting through this in the fastest, healthiest way possible, so am starting to build in habits, well-being focus, and gratitude practices. I am growing more comfortable in owning and knowing my story and already benefiting from putting it out there to my Energy Hype Squad during this season.

In fact, in building my Energy Hype Squad, I reached out to my dear friend Meg, who I introduced earlier in the book. She reminded me how supported, loved, and strong I am and offered such a rich perspective. "You are absolutely right. You do have this. You have been strengthening your boat by writing this book and listening to the stories of others as you prepare for this storm. Please remember that 'a smooth sea never made for a skilled sailor.' You and I both know you will come out of this storm with that same Big Energy you went into it with and the number of women who will gain strength from you and your story gives me chills. I love you and will be riding this storm out with you."

And that, my friends, is how we build our boats and captain the seas together so we are able to harness and invest our energy to survive, thrive, transform, and grow!

**WHAT COMES NEXT?**
Several months ago, while working, I took a quick break to grab a coffee in my kitchen. I had been hours into working on a new Bring Your Big Energy workshop that I was developing, and I had this intense feeling in my body. It literally felt electric, y'all—I am not lying—and at first, I thought it with anxiety or stress.

I put a hand on my heart and stomach to understand more and quickly discovered it was actually a feeling of pure joy. Another rush of intensity ran through me, making me wish I had twenty hours in a day to coach and create transformational programming, and I realized that is what it is all about. Trust me when I tell you I have never had that feeling, professionally speaking, and wished I could bottle it up. This type of living into your purpose and passion ignites that spark and creates that currency. This is what I deserve and what you deserve—the ignition of something joyous, meaningful, and bigger than us.

I hope that these stories, insights, practices, and reflection techniques have helped you as you continue to explore clarity in your journey and undergo your energy transformation.

As I leave you, I want to remind you of a few things.

## PRACTICE AND PERSISTENCE

Persistence is key for continued momentum and ongoing energy. To do this, we need to continue to practice these tools and exercises we have discussed along our journey here.

Persistence is all about continuous, determined application toward your goals. In practice, persistence involves consistently showing up, putting in the work, and persevering through challenges and setbacks. You will need a resilient attitude and a commitment to improvement, even when progress may seem slow or difficult. We will all have days that we fall. We just need to get back up.

The trick is knowing that it's going to be hard but doing it anyway. I do this when I don't feel like running. I make an agreement with myself to get on the treadmill and just try a bit of walking. Eventually, though, once I get warmed up and start to gain momentum, motivation kicks in, and the next thing I know I am three miles into a good sweaty run.

We talked about the importance of daily progress to be sure you are making small steps to your goals. And remember that even some progress is better than none. A crappy workout is better than none. A crappy chapter is a chapter started. Just keep moving.

Don't forget mini-celebrations: small things like a bubble bath, getting your nails done, going to bed with a good book, and so on. They don't need to be huge; just keep those "joy bombs" coming.

Each small step taken toward a goal contributes to the overall progress and eventual achievement of success. As Robert Collier, self-help superstar, says, "Success is the sum of small efforts repeated day in and day out."[1] Having the plans in place to ladder up to the goal and tracking them are amazing ways to keep moving forward.

**YOU ARE NOT ALONE**
It takes community and support for us to thrive. People who lean into their communities are known to be happier and to live longer. In fact, according to Harvard School of Public Health, across numerous studies they performed, they found that people with strong social connections live longer and healthier lives. On the flip side, the National Library of Medicine reported on a study that found when multidimensional assessments of social relationships were considered, those who are socially isolated see their odds of mortality increased by 91 percent. In times of transformation, having a community to support and advocate for you is critical for your success.[2]

So build and nurture your Energy Hype Squad, and it will pay off in dividends. Make a point to do accountability and wellness check-ins along the way, and always do a yearly reflection on your vision and goals. My hope is that you are able to reread this book multiple times, and each year, and I will be a partner on your journey.

I am rooting for you!

If you are looking to continue this work in more depth, you can always check out my website to inquire about individual coaching or find cities where my events and workshops are offered. While I may not always have individual coaching availability, my workshops and group coaching sessions, both in person and online, are a great way to leverage the SPARK process in community with others. You can always shoot me a note at StaceyK@BringYourBigEnergy.com or pick up the phone and give me a call if you and your team are looking for SPARK customized sessions. Lastly, I also have a team of amazing coaches I partner with if I am unable to help you.

If you need to stay local, leverage this book and resources to lead your own mini session at home with yummy snacks and zero distractions during an intentional time.

Partnering one on one with a coach, regardless who they are, is an absolute game-changer as you work through transformation, career transitions, or to up-level your strengths to be the best version of you. A great coach will help you continue on this journey by holding space for you, asking you provocative questions, helping you model and design what could be, and challenging you to consider fresh perspectives in a safe and trusted environment where you can experiment, learn, and grow!

One of the best coaches I ever had helped me realize that I needed to take a break and spend time reflecting on my life and nurturing myself. With her help, I began thinking bigger and bolder on what could be next for me, which ultimately saved my life and gave me the confidence to take a path unknown but full of passion, excitement, and meaning. For me, having a coach has also been critical to my success, and seeing the power of it actually moved me into this work. She holds me accountable to a larger vision, calls me out on negative limiting self-talk, and refuses to believe my fears or the old stories I tell myself.

I highly recommend coaching and am proud to share that I have helped hundreds of clients see amazing results, some of which include: promotions and career advancement, deciding to pursue and getting accepted to further educations like an MBA program, creating more time to do things they love with better balance and more peace, getting new jobs, winning awards, launching small businesses, removing lifelong self-imposed limiting beliefs, increasing confidence and self-awareness, and building the ability to stop running and instead present their most authentic self. In the end, while clients put in the effort, I'm right there alongside them as a partner and catalyst, helping them reach their goals and achieve their biggest dreams!

Truly transformational work requires dedication and commitment. When working with a coach, you should be eager and determined to create a new life and move beyond feeling stuck. By embracing new perspectives, committing to regular sessions (just as you would with your doctor or dentist), and being inspired by the future you can achieve through full engagement, you set yourself up for success. So the real question is not whether you need coaching but whether you want it and are ready to change your life.

Isn't it worth it to transform your life completely?

**BUT WHEN YOU ARE ALONE—WORK IT!**
Keep prioritizing yourself, setting intentions, and believing in the endless world of abundant possibilities! Continue to increase your self-awareness, understanding what energizes you and what drains you. Pay attention, because it matters.

I hope this book helped you get energized and hyped you up. I hope you are leaving me from a place of radiating your own amazing authentic power. I also hope you pay it forward and become the energy magnet you are called to be through inspiring and encouraging others. Please share what you learned with your community, and please tag me on all the socials at @BringYourBigEnergy or use #BringYourBigEnergy to join my Energy Hype Squad!

It is time. We have spent too long doing the things we think we are supposed to do, to chase the things we are supposed to want, and to secure the things we are supposed to have. And maybe, just maybe, none of that matters. What matters is that we are showing up. We are listening to our inner selves and chasing what success looks like for us.

By pursuing what ignites us, we align more deeply with the legacy we aspire to leave.

Remember, you are uniquely positioned to bring extraordinary things to the world. There are no carbon copies. The world needs you and the Big Energy you bring. When negative self-talk tries to convince you that everything has already been done or said, remember it has never been done in your unique way. Your story is one only you can tell. By stifling yourself, coasting, avoiding, and numbing, you lose your way.

What if every single day you just put one foot in front of the other to transform into the best version of yourself, making this one life you have to live the best possible life it can be? Bring your Big Energy. The world needs you.

# ACKNOWLEDGMENTS

---

When they say, "It takes a village," they aren't kidding. Without mine, I could never have brought Bring Your Big Energy to life. I am profoundly honored and blessed by how my village rallied around me. From the early days of concept, with over four hundred Energy Hype Squad members, to the final presale campaign, where nearly two hundred Bring Your Big Energy Ambassadors cheered me on, helped make key decisions, and generously financially supported this book—I am forever grateful for each and every one of you.

**To the storytellers within the book:** It was an absolute honor to become immersed in your stories and to have your trust to share them with the world in hopes that others may feel connected and inspired by the seasons you've all experienced. When I started this journey, I thought it would be about my story and my perspective, but as I spoke with each of you, the book came alive. It couldn't have existed without your vulnerability and wisdom:

Adele Myszenski, Amber Prong, Angie Creger, April Hipps, Kim Willis, Cheryl Crab, Dave Moerlein, Derek Pflum, Erin

Wiley, Jennifer King, Karen Godwin, Meghan Riedl, Monica Curtis, Monica Dressler, Sara Bonzheim, and Suzanne Roske.

**To my subject matter experts and pen name participants:** Thank you for allowing me to use your stories and subject matter expertise under pen names to protect your privacy and vulnerabilities while still sharing your valuable insights. Your contributions have been instrumental in shaping this book and making it resonate deeply with readers. I extend my deepest gratitude and am forever grateful for your contributions to the heart of this project. Your voices, though veiled, will resonate with readers and inspire them profoundly.

**To my Bring Your Big Energy Ambassadors:** The support from you, my author community, turned this dream into reality. You empowered me to share my story, the inspiring stories of others, and my insights with the world. Your engagement throughout the process ensured that readers would find deep value in these pages, connect with the exercises, and appreciate a visually compelling cover. None of this would have been possible without you:

Adele Myszenski, Alana Reome, Alicia Roberts, Alicia Wilson, Amanda Pirrami, Ami Sirlin, Amy Hess, Amy Kerschbaum, Amy Lyczak, Amy Perry, Amy Scroggs, Andrea Slawski, Angela Shires, Angie Creger, Anne Bresler, Anthony Derosa, Antonella Grimaldi, April Hipps, Ashlee Piper, Asja Trumic, Barb O'Connell, Basil Wuson, Beah Tagani, Becca Pusta, Beth Leverton, Beth Reed, Bethann Macioci, Betsy Broglin, Brandy Bugni, Brenda Fridman, Bridget Drzewicki, Brienne Warden, Carin Meyer, Carly Forsthoefel, Catherine Connelly, Catherine Ornekian, Chanel Ashkar, Cheryl Crabb, Cheryl

Mills, Cheryl Zammataro, Chrissy Greenblatt, Christa Festa, Christina Johnson, Christine Carroll, Christine Rush, Chrystal Roessler, Cleary Puchley, Colleen Moerlein, Corinna St.Aubin, Dana Garbolino, Daniel Assisi, Daniela Zahab-Palmer, Dawn Kilarski, Deanna Badiru, Deanna Sypula, Deb Cantrell, Dee Shah, Deena Ashford Gardner, Dina Mestel, Elana Chan, Eleni Vrahnos, Eric Koester, Eric Kulongowski, Erin Maten, Erin Stacer, Erin Wiley, Faith Garbolino, Fatima Rider, Hailey Jones, Heather Martin, Heather Powers, Holley Beasley, Jack O'connor, Jacqui Maroccia, James Mcgee, Jamie Furst, Jason Witt, Jaye Mccormick, Jen Almeida, Jen Lutz, Jenn Ader, Jenna Kerschbaum, Jennifer Hahn, Jennifer Baldwin, Jennifer Culp, Jennifer Haran, Jennifer King, Jennifer Puzsar, Jessica Drury, Jim Cleven, Jodi Beintema, Jodie Roden, Johanna Lara, Judy Shumway, Julie Currie, Julie Malloure, Julie Mattison, Kajal Brazwell, Kamaron Moore, Kara Gabay, Karen Godwin, Karen Granata, Karen Kazarian, Karen Morris, Karen O'connor, Kari Wegienka, Karri Valot Rijo, Kate Sochacki, Katie Wilson, Kelly Ponder, Kelly Zimmermann, Kim App, Kim Dahring, Kim West, Kimberly Freij, Kimberly Kaminski, Kristen Strychar, Kristin Stoops, Lacie Sandstrom, Laura Anne Vansickle, Laura Armstrong, Laura Perkins, Laura Rybicki, Laura Zuidema, Lauren Hamerink, Laurie Bevevino, Leslie Cardenas, Lindsay Schultz, Lindsey Adams, Lindsey Levich, Lisa Mccausland, Lisa Mcintyre, Lisa Sammon, Lori Tabb, Maria Mooney, Marie Szuts, Marinela Zgourov, Marissa Layman, Mary Kay Pflum, Meg Riedl, Melissa Dewey, Melissa Grusche, Michele Kimmet, Michele Pisarik, Michelle Dell, Michelle Polletta, Mike Maten, Milea Vislosky, Mindy Dolan, Monica Curtis, Monica Davis, Monica Dressler, Nancy Mccloud, Natalie Adames, Natalie Green, Nicole Obeidi, Nicole Gulinazzo,

Nicole Lipkin, Nicole Schwartz, Nikki Patterson, Nina Graham, Pia Mailhot-Leichter, Rachel Levy, Ryan O'connor, Saloni Janveja, Sara Bonzheim, Sara Scurfield, Sarah Green, Sarah Devereaux, Sarah Hollingsworth, Sarah Schleicher, Sean O'connor, Seema Vashi Garg, Selin Song, Shelly Lubbers, Sherry Becker, Stacey Woodman, Stefanie Porter, Stephanie Lowther, Stephanie Rife, Susan Lavington, Susan Pulaski, Suzanne Roske, Tamara Besco, Tara Stone, Taylor Smith, Terry Puchley, Theresa Culp, Theresa Vitale, Tiffani Gallico, and Tiffany Krogman.

**To my beta and heavy pen readers:** For letting me put my work out there in those initial days when it was terrifying and I felt so raw sharing it all. Thank you for your feedback, your honesty, and your countless collective hours of reading and editing so I could bring my readers the best experience possible. Our joint dedication to do so makes this book the magic it is. Forever thankful for you:

Adele Myszenski, Bridget Drzewicki, Julie Currie, Kim App, Laura Anne, Marie Szuts, Michelle Polletta, and Stephanie Rife.

**To my writing and editing team and fellow authors at Manuscripts:** Thank you for sustaining my spirit on the days I felt I couldn't continue, when the rough drafts seemed insurmountable, and for helping me transform my cancer recurrence news into the spark for a potential second book. If *Bring Your Pink Energy* ever becomes a reality, I hope you will walk this journey with me. To Eric Koester for giving us all a stage to share our work with the world, to my developmental editor David Grandouiller, my structural editor Angela

Mitchell, my revisions editor Frances Chiu, my marketing partner Jacques Moolman, my instruction wrangler Kristy Elam, and our amazing instructor Shanna Heath. To my fellow authors, wherever we connected in the process, Dar Dixon, Charles Moore, Catherine Connelly, Jennifer Clark, Victor Barnes, Alix Rowland, Heather Powers, Mauricio Velasquez, Johannes Chudoba, and Pia Leichter.

**To my parents:** I don't know how it all ends, but I do know how it all began for me—with the two of you. How did I get so lucky? You have been there every step of the way and every single time I was building a dream. You always made me believe it was possible, encouraged me, cried with me, and pushed me to keep going because "That's what Culps do." I am forever grateful for the lessons of resilience, grit, optimism, and dreaming that you taught me. Without you, there would have been no big dreams, resources needed to make them happen, or the motivation to keep going. So, thank you from the bottom of my heart. And, yes, Dad, you're still getting the first cut of the first million I make from this book. I know you're holding on to that IOU from eighth grade.

**To the Kules Family of Five:** Every day I am in awe of the life we have built, the people we continue to become, and the blessings we have all around us. Big Energy as a concept was born from the calling to help others live their best life, but the truth is, without all of your support, I would never be living mine. Thank you for always entertaining my wild Big Energy ideas and adventures, for celebrating big for any little reason, for chasing adventure because nothing is worse than being ordinary, and for sticking with me through countless hours of writing and revisions. Thank you for not once questioning my dream but pouring gasoline on it because of your blind belief that anything is possible for me—for us. Grace, your calm and even energy always reminds me to slow down, believe in myself, and celebrate all I have accomplished. Maddie, my own personal high-energy pump-up squad who I am pretty sure believes I could perform on the biggest stage in the world and kill it. Lottie, for your lightness, laughter, and perspective that it is all always going to be all right and that anything is possible as long as we are together. Eric, for never doubting me, always believing in me, and building this beautiful life with me on the back of a cocktail napkin so many years ago. I love and cherish you all.

# Notes

**INTRODUCTION**
1. Ernesto Scherer, "Tony Robbins: The Pain of Changing Yourself (Motivational Video)," Ernesto Scherer, June 20, 2017, 00:15:28, www.youtube.com/watch?v=l1QQ0uPG-H8.

**CHAPTER 1. HOW DID YOU GET HERE, AND WHERE IS HERE?**
1. Ernesto Scherer, "Tony Robbins: The Pain of Changing Yourself (Motivational Video)," Ernesto Scherer, June 20, 2017, 00:15:28, www.youtube.com/watch?v=l1QQ0uPG-H8.

2. E. Beth Hemphill, "Uncomfortable (but Necessary) Conversations About Burnout," Gallup, December 6, 2022, https://www.gallup.com/workplace/406232/uncomfortable-necessary-conversations-burnout.aspx#.

3. Shradha Dinesh and Kim Parker, "More than 4 in 10 US Workers Don't Take All Their Paid Time Off," Pew Research Center, August 10, 2023, https://www.pewresearch.org/short-reads/2023/08/10/more-than-4-in-10-u-s-workers-dont-take-all-their-paid-time-off/.

4. Kimberly Willis, *Walk through Fire: A Survivor's Story* (Michigan: ASA Publishing Corporation, 2019).

5. American Psychological Association, "Trauma," American Psychological Association website, accessed September 3, 2024, https://www.apa.org/topics/trauma.

6   Joseph R. Novello, *The Myth of More: And Other Lifetraps That Sabotage the Happiness You Deserve* (New Jersey: Paulist Press, 2001), 177.

**CHAPTER 2. SPARK ENERGY TRANSFORMATION PROCESS**

1   John C. Maxwell, *The 15 Invaluable Laws of Growth* (New York: Center Street, 2022), 156.

2   Martin Luther King Jr., *Where Do We Go from Here: Chaos or Community?* (New York: Harper & Row, 1967).

**CHAPTER 3. SELF-REFLECTION**

1   Danny Arguetty, "The Sound of Silent Breakfast," Kripalu, accessed September 3, 2024, https://kripalu.org/resources/sound-silent-breakfast.

2   Joseph H. Arguinchona and Prasanna Tadi, "Neuroanatomy, Reticular Activating System," National Library of Medicine, accessed September 3, 2024, https://www.ncbi.nlm.nih.gov/books/NBK549835/.

3   Mind Journal, "There Is a Voice That Doesn't Use Words. Listen," X @ TheMindsJournal, January 9, 2021, https://x.com/TheMindsJournal/status/1348155109944000513.

4   Maharishi Mahesh Yogi, "Transcendental Meditation: Mechanics of the Technique (Maharishi Mahesh Yogi)," Maharishi International University, April 3, 2009, 00:02:49, https://www.youtube.com/watch?v=fbX5eNAbpeo.

5   David Von Drehle, *The Book of Charlie: Wisdom from the Remarkable American Life of a 109-Year-Old Man* (New York: Simon & Schuster, 2023), 15.

6   Harold S. Kushner, *When All You've Ever Wanted Isn't Enough* (New York: Summit Books, 1986), 160–161.

7   Arthur C. Brooks, *From Strength to Strength: Finding Success, Happiness, and Deep Purpose in the Second Half of Life* (London: Portfolio, 2022), 39–45.

**CHAPTER 4. PURPOSE**

1   Ari Weinzweig, "The Recipe for Visioning," The Great Game of Business, August 11, 2022, https://www.greatgame.com/podcast/episode91.

2   Jim Rohn, "Jim Rohn Life Lesson: The 7 Fundamentals of Success | Jim Rohn Motivational Video 2024," Motivation Alchemists, March 18, 2024, 16:33, https://www.youtube.com/watch?v=YXN72-14dJQ.

3   Simon Bell, "The Wheel of Life," Mind Tools, accessed September 3, 2024, https://www.mindtools.com/ak6jd6w/the-wheel-of-life.

4   Brené Brown, *The Gifts of Imperfection: Let Go of Who You Think You're Supposed to Be and Embrace Who You Are* (Minnesota: Hazelden, 2010), 96.

5   George T. Doran, "There's a SMART Way to Write Management's Goals and Objectives," *Journal of Management Review* Vol. 70 (November 1981): 35–36, https://community.mis.temple.edu/mis0855002fall2015/files/2015/10/S.M.A.R.T-Way-Management-Review.pdf.

6   Jack Flynn, "15+ Essential Goal-Setting Statistics [2023]: The Importance of Setting Goals" Zippia, December 11, 2023, https://www.zippia.com/advice/goal-setting-statistics/#.

7   Gary W. Keller and Jay Papasan, *The ONE Thing: The Surprisingly Simple Truth behind Extraordinary Results* (Oregon: Bard Press, 2013), 117.

8   Rachel Hollis, "Would You Commit to 90 Days to Change the Rest of Your Life? 'Last 90 Days' Challenge Sign-Ups," Rachel Hollis, September 25, 2017, 00:26:23, https://www.facebook.com/thechicsite/videos/10155575063056259.

9   Ayoa, "Tony Buzan on the Origins of Mind Mapping," Aoya, October 27, 2010, 00:5:23, https://www.youtube.com/watch?v=2LX3peWpxV8.

## CHAPTER 5. ABANDON (AND UNPLUG)

1   Statista Research Department, "Number of Participants in Triathlons in the United States from 2010 to 2023," Statista, accessed September 3, 2024, https://www.statista.com/statistics/191339/participants-in-triathlons-in-the-us-since-2006.

2   Cheryl Crabb, *The Other Side of Sanctuary: A Novel* (New York: Adelaide Books, 2019).

3   Shirzad Chamine, "About," Positive Intelligence, accessed September 3, 2024, https://www.positiveintelligence.com/about/.

4   Richard Schwartz, "About," IFS Institute, accessed September 3, 2024, https://ifs-institute.com/about-us.

5   Muhammad Asif, "Nothing to Fear but Fear Itself: How the Fear of Failure Is Holding You Back in Business," *Forbes*, October 10, 2022, https://www.forbes.com/councils/forbesbusinesscouncil/2022/10/10/nothing-to-fear-but-fear-itself-how-the-fear-of-failure-is-holding-you-back-in-business/.

6   Frank Lewis Dyer and Thomas Commerford Martin, *Edison: His Life and Inventions* (New York: Harper, 1910), 207.

7   Dr. Tilisa Thibodeaux, "Learner's Mindset Explained," Learners Mindset, February 5, 2021, 00:34:38, https://www.youtube.com/watch?v=HAtzyabZkfI.

8   Robert Kegan and Lisa Laskow Lahey, *Immunity to Change: How to Overcome It and Unlock the Potential in Yourself and Your Organization* (Massachusetts: Harvard Business Review Press, 2009).

9   Stephen R. Covey, *The 7 Habits of Highly Effective People*, (UK: Simon & Schuster, 1989), 19.

10  Bill Burnett and Dave Evans, *Designing Your Life: How to Build a Well-Lived, Joyful Life* (New York: Knopf, 2016), x and xxix.

11  Timber Hawkeye, *The Opposite of Namaste* (Australia: Hawkeye Publishers, 2022).

12  Matshona Dhliwayo, "You don't excel by conforming to society. You excel by conforming to your higher self," Matshona Dhliwayo's Facebook, accessed September 3, 2024, https://www.facebook.com/photo.php?fbid=2241191572763592&id=1995238897358862&set=a.1997628227119929&locale=ku_TR.

13  M.S. Oitzl, "Avoidance Conditioning," Science Direct, accessed September 3, 2024, https://www.sciencedirect.com/topics/agricultural-and-biological-sciences/avoidance-conditioning.

14  J-H Krannich, P. Weyers, S. Lueger, H. Faller, C. Schimmer, P. Deeg, O. Elert, and R. Leyh, "The Short- and Long-Term Motivational Effects of a Patient Education Programme for Patients with Coronary Artery Bypass Grafting," *Rehabilitation (Stuttg)* Vol. 47, 4 (August 2008): 219–225, doi: 10.1055/s-2007-1004598.

## CHAPTER 6. RESULTS

1  Harvard Health Medical School, "Why You Should Move—Even Just a Little—throughout the Day," *Heart Health* (blog), *Harvard Medical School*, July 14, 2023, https://www.health.harvard.edu/heart-health/why-you-should-move-even-just-a-little-throughout-the-day.

2  ASN Staff, "How to Boost Mental Health through Better Nutrition," American Society for Nutrition, April 18, 2023, https://nutrition.org/how-to-boost-mental-health-through-better-nutrition/.

3  Raza Ahmad, MD, "How Much Water Do You Need Each Day?" Penn Medicine, May 20, 2015, https://www.pennmedicine.org/updates/blogs/health-and-wellness/2015/may/how-much-water-do-you-need-each-day#.

4  Alana I. Mendelsohn, "Creatures of Habit: The Neuroscience of Habit and Purposeful Behavior," National Library of Medicine, June 1, 2019, https://www.ncbi.nlm.nih.gov/pmc/articles/PMC6701929/.

5  James Clear, "Quotes," JamesClear.com, accessed September 30, 2024, https://jamesclear.com/quotes/every-action-you-take-is-a-vote-for-the-type-of-person-you-wish-to-become-no-single-instance-will-transform-your-beliefs-but-as-the-votes-build-up-so-does-the-evidence-of-your-new-identity.

6  James Clear, *Atomic Habits: An Easy and Proven Way to Build Good Habits and Break Bad Ones* (New York: Avery, 2019).

7  Jeff Shore, "These 10 Peter Drucker Quotes May Change Your World," NBC News, September 16, 2014, https://www.nbcnews.com/id/wbna56060818.

8  Barrett Wissman, "An Accountability Partner Makes You Vastly More Likely to Succeed," Entrepreneur, March 20, 2018, https://www.

entrepreneur.com/leadership/an-accountability-partner-makes-you-vastly-more-likely-to/310062.

9   John Coleman, "Reviewing Cynefin—Weaving Sense Making into the Fabric of Our World with Dave Snowden," Agility Island, October 5, 2021, 00:55:54, https://www.youtube.com/watch?v=qLAyXnUx_TU.

10  Gretchen Rubin, "The Happiness Project Explained," Gretchen Rubin, January 15, 2024, 00:01:42, https://www.youtube.com/watch?v=z5BwXRWdbK4.

11  Ralph Waldo Emerson, selected and edited by Joel Porte, Emerson in His Journals Nov. 1842 entry, (Massachusetts: Harvard University Press, 1982), 294–295.

12  Ernst T. Bohlmeijer, Jannis T. Kraiss, Philip Watkins, and Marijke Schotanus-Dijkstra, "Promoting Gratitude as a Resource for Sustainable Mental Health: Results of a 3-Armed Randomized Controlled Trial up to 6 Months Follow-Up," *Journal of Happiness Studies: An Interdisciplinary Forum on Subjective Well-Being, Vol. 22, 3*, (May 2020), 1011–1032, https://doi.org/10.1007/s10902-020-00261-5.

13  Jo A. Iodice, John M. Malouff, and Nicola S. Schutte, "The Association between Gratitude and Depression: A Meta-Analysis." *International Journal of Depression and Anxiety*, Vol.4, 1, (June 2021): doi.org/10.23937/2643-4059/1710024.

## CHAPTER 7. KINETIC ENERGY

1   Brené Brown, *Rising Strong: The Reckoning. The Rumble. The Revolution* (New York: Random House, 2015). 183.

2   Malcolm Gladwell, *Outliers: The Story of Success* (New York: Back Bay Books, 2011). 42.

3   Marwa Azab, "The History of Imposter Syndrome," *Psychology Today*, August 22, 2022, https://www.psychologytoday.com/us/blog/neuroscience-in-everyday-life/202308/the-history-of-imposter-syndrome.

4   Kess Eruteya, "You're Not an Imposter. You're Actually Pretty Amazing," *Harvard Business Review*, January 3, 2022, https://hbr.org/2022/01/youre-not-an-imposter-youre-actually-pretty-amazing.

5   Luciana Paulise, "75 percent of Women Executives Experience Imposter Syndrome in the Workplace," *Forbes*, August 3, 2023, https://www.forbes.com/sites/lucianapaulise/2023/03/08/75-of-women-executives-experience-imposter-syndrome-in-the-workplace/.

6   Tara Brach, "Article: The Power of Radical Acceptance: Healing Trauma through the Integration of Buddhist Meditation and Psychotherapy," Tara Brach, July 1, 2011, https://www.tarabrach.com/trauma/.

7   Quoteresearch, "Quote Origin: Comparison Is the Thief of Joy," Quote Investigator, February 6, 2021, https://quoteinvestigator.com/2021/02/06/thief-of-joy/?.

8   Tom Peters, "The Brand Called You," *Fast Company Premium* (blog), *Fast Company*, accessed September 3, 2024, https://www.fastcompany.com/28905/brand-called-you.

9   Center for Career Development: Princeton University, "Developing Your Elevator Pitch," Center for Career Development: Princeton University, accessed September 3, 2024, https://careerdevelopment.princeton.edu/guides/networking/developing-your-elevator-pitch.

## CHAPTER 8. BRING YOUR BIG "LEADER" ENERGY

1   PR Newswire, "New DDI Research: 57 Percent of Employees Quit Because of Their Boss," PR Newswire, December 9, 2019, https://www.prnewswire.com/news-releases/new-ddi-research-57-percent-of-employees-quit-because-of-their-boss-300971506.html.

## CHAPTER 9. EMBRACE YOUR EPIC ENERGY

1   Robert Collier, *Riches within Your Reach: The Law of the Higher Potential* (New York: Robert Collier Publishing, 1947), 205.

2   Yang Claire Yang, Courtney Boen, Karen Gerken, Ting Li, Kristen Schorpp, and Kathleen Mullan Harris, "Social Relationships and Physiological Determinants of Longevity across the Human Life Span," National Library of Medicine, accessed September 3, 2024, https://pubmed.ncbi.nlm.nih.gov/26729882/.